NEWS NOW

BEING A TV JOURNALIST

Sudesna Ghosh

Collins

First published in India in 2016 by Collins
An imprint of HarperCollins *Publishers*

HarperCollins Publishers India, Cyber City, Building 10-A, Gurugram,
Haryana-122002, India
www.harpercollins.co.in

P-ISBN: 978-93-5177-937-7
E-ISBN: 978-93-5177-938-4

2 4 6 8 10 9 7 5 3 1

Typeset in 11/14 Requiem at
Manipal Digital Systems, Manipal

Printed and bound at
MicroPrints India, New Delhi

MIX
Paper
FSC FSC® C218906

This product is made of FSC®-certified and other controlled material.

HarperCollins Publishers, Macken House, 39/40 Mayor Street
Upper, Dublin 1, D01 C9W8, Ireland

To
Ma and Baba

CONTENTS

A Note for the Readers

'So what are you going to be when you grow up?' Haven't we all been asked that question? Some decades ago, your answer would probably have been one of the following: lawyer, doctor, scientist or engineer. Fast forward to 2016 and you find a bunch of enthusiastic youngsters who are bombarded with enough career options to keep them exploring forever.

Remember how Nandita, the lead character in the movie *Peepli Live*, was a newsreader? Well, being a newsreader is just one of the many roles that you can fill in the modern TV newsroom. Being a part of the broadcast world is not just about having a perfect accent in front of the camera. As you read *Beyond the Deadline*, you'll realize that there are many more people behind the scenes who work together tirelessly to bring you the news shows that you watch on TV.

When I joined *The Telegraph* as a print journalist in 2009, everything was new to me. I didn't even know the difference between working on the desk and working as a reporter. I also had no idea how pages were made per day. By the time I left the organization, I had learnt it all. Even then, I wished I had done more research about the field before I'd joined. It's always good to be prepared.

That's why I decided to write this book. That's why I spent hours talking to top journalists in the field and some experienced professors too. Along with that, I read any material I could get my hands on to make sure that this book serves you well. I want you to get a feel of what you will experience in the newsroom. If you aren't sure that you would like to be a TV journalist, I hope this book will help you take a decision. So here's to getting ready for the journey to become the next Barkha Dutt or Rajdeep Sardesai!

INTRODUCTION

TVs are everywhere, these days. At home, in the office—sometimes, even in shops—it seems like there's always a television lurking somewhere, blaring the news if nothing else. You could say that the idiot box, as we have come to call it, is now intrinsic to our survival. That probably explains why so many people can't wait to be a part of that world. Ever dreamed of being one of those who read out the news to the entire nation? Or a cameraman, risking life and limb to bring viewers images in the midst of a fire or a tsunami? Or even the editor, who gets to choose the most impactful stories? If so, this book will guide you to that dream. But before that, let's back up a little. If you want to be a part of the Indian television industry, you should probably know how it came to take the form it currently has. Let's take a quick history lesson.

Did you know that people in India could not even watch television until 1959? At the time, television sets were only visible at technology fairs or at exhibitions of that nature. That changed at a UNESCO (the United Nations Educational, Scientific and Cultural Organization) conference in Delhi that year, where Indian representatives requested access to video- and TV-related technology, to be used for educational purposes.

Granting their request, the United States government, in collaboration with the electronics company Philips built a studio at the All India Radio (AIR) premises. The first television set was inaugurated on 15 September 1959.

What did they show on TV?

Following suggestions made by UNESCO, tele-clubs came into the picture. Each tele-club had a television set that was available for club members. Two years later, a TV programme for college and university students was launched and found to be very effective as well. Almost twenty television sets were set up in villages around Delhi, and each tele-club had about 150 members. The telecast was aired only twice a week—for only an hour each time—and the content was limited to documentaries and informational programmes that focused on citizen's duties and rights, community health, traffic and road sense. The response was positive, leading the government to increase telecast services in 1965. This meant bringing in some fun entertainment shows too.

Independence Day, 1965, was a historic moment for the country. From that day on, for the first time, the government began to telecast a full hour-long programme regularly. As TV then progressed from being a luxury item to a device for daily entertainment, Indians saw about 22,000 imported television sets entering the nation—not counting those for community purposes. Soon, Indian films and music programmes were introduced as well, and a limited number of old US and British shows were shown sometimes as well. The *Ramayana* and *Mahabharata* were the first major TV series produced indigenously and later telecast in the '80s. By 1976, the government had launched Doordarshan, the national television network. Advertising arrived after that, leading to the development of content beyond documentaries and informational programmes: soap operas, comedy shows, dramas, quiz shows and musical entertainment. The 1980s was the era of Doordarshan, and those who lived through it might still remember the serials of that era; *Hum Log* (1984), *Wagle Ki Duniya* (1988) and *Buniyaad* (1986), to name a few.

In 1975, the Indian government carried out a test to study the possibilities of satellite-based television. SITE (Satellite Instructional Television Experiment) was used to telecast programmes for about four hours each day. The content mainly consisted of education for school children, out-of-school education, agricultural issues, planning and national integration. Based on the results, the government created its own satellite service called INSAT, which was launched in 1982.

The entry of international satellite television was a watershed moment for the Indian broadcasting industry. The big year was 1991, when the country watched the coverage of the Gulf War on CNN. Three months later, Hong Kong–based Star TV began broadcasting five channels in India, using the ASIASAT-1 satellite. There was continued growth leading to the launch of a number of viewing options between 1991 and 1994. The list included Zee TV—our first Hindi satellite channel.

Hello, TV news!

Newspapers had already been in existence for a while, but broadcast news was only just beginning to grow in the early 1990s. The difference in the history of print media and that of broadcast is in their development. Print journalism evolved from a process. Think about it this way: Printing evolved from the process of manual transcription of manuscripts. It began with paper. Broadcast journalism, on the other hand, was born from technology. Inventions such as the telegraph, telephone, radio, Internet and television weren't made for broadcast journalism, but people figured out how to adapt these media to journalism. That's why broadcast is a younger, innovatively created medium.

Given its recent beginnings, TV news has evolved enormously in a very short span of time. Consider, for example, the difference between a news bulletin in the 1980s or '90s and those of today. Do you remember the drab studio backgrounds and the newsreaders just sitting there, reading out the news with only the occasional video clip and almost no on-screen graphics? The digitalization of the newsroom—computers, sophisticated software and the like—has transformed the landscape completely. Today, software like Octopus or iNews can control just about everything—the script, the edited visual package, studio and anchor links, production cues, duration details and more. Additionally, the production control room (PCR) operations are completely digitalized these days too. This has not only done away with the problem of human error, but stories can be moved up and down the sequence of stories at the click of the producer's mouse button.

Print news vs TV news

There are a number of mediums these days through which news can be delivered to an audience. Already, news transmission through social media platforms (like Twitter and Facebook) is gaining ground. A survey conducted by Weber Shandwick had this to say: All TV journalists being surveyed reported spending more than four hours online every day for work. Thirty per cent of the 130 journalists surveyed said that they first research their stories online. Nonetheless, for a very long time, there were only two major options for news consumption—print or broadcast.

Let us now take a closer look at the differences in the required skill sets for these two mediums. To begin with, there is more editing involved with print. Newspapers and magazines edit for clarity, fairness and accuracy. They also edit to make sure that every article maintains the media house's style (capitalization rules, italics and the like). In broadcast journalism, on the other hand, it isn't just the text that is being edited. Even though it can seem like the reporter or anchor is speaking off the cuff, aspects such as news angles and footage are often planned in advance. The broadcast editing process usually involves video editing and editing of the script as well; but when a news segment is coming to you live, there is no scope for any editing.

Print and broadcast news stories also differ in length and pace. The average radio news story is thirty seconds long. The average television news story is one minute and thirty seconds long. The average print news piece can vary in length, and the reader dictates the pace in this case, not the journalist.

When one considers the impact of broadcast and print media, one should keep in mind that they are also different in terms of how much the audience can retain and recall. Your TV can be on and still be ignored. In contrast, print media cannot be consumed absent-mindedly. For example, a person can turn on the TV and be busy with other things like making dinner or checking their phone for WhatsApp messages. But when you are reading the newspaper, you have to be focusing far more intently.

These mediums also influence the audience in different ways. Broadcast media is presented by anchors and reporters who can be studied for their tone of voice, physical build, gender and attire. These features influence the audience's perception of how authentic or accurate the news is. People watching TV news form perceptions immediately based on what they see or hear—similar to meeting people in our daily lives. Everyone has a favourite anchor that they trust, and come what may, they will make time to catch their show. Newspaper readers do not see or hear the reporter. Only the byline gives away the reporter's gender. Only one factor can influence the reader—the writing style.

So you want to be on TV?

The fleeting yet powerful impact of broadcast news is tempting. You could be the face of your channel and become a well-known name in every household. Or you could be behind the scenes, quietly but urgently editing scripts and footage. You could also be the one reporting from dangerous areas, enjoying the thrill of being a part of big events.

There are many more roles that one can adopt in the newsroom, and we will get to those in detail a little further along in this book; but before that, it is important to understand that television isn't just about the person you see on your screen. There's a lot going on behind the camera. By the time you're done with this book, I hope to have offered you some insights on how the news is brought to you so that nothing comes as a surprise once you finally get there.

Also, at the end of this book you will get to meet some well-known faces—eight major journalists who have been doing amazing things in this industry. Read about the challenges they faced in their journalism careers. Learn important lessons from them. Get valuable advice. By the time you finish reading their stories you'll find yourself inspired and ready to be a part of the newsroom.

1

INSIDE THE NEWSROOM

A newsroom, especially one in a television channel, is a place of chaos, frayed tempers and last-minute surprises. Even on a slow news day it is rare to find people calmly seated at their workstations—there's always a buzz in the air. In a way, this explains why there have been countless films, books and TV shows centred upon the newsroom; the setting naturally lends itself to a lot of excitement and drama.

However, as a viewer, one only sees the poker-faced anchor on the television screen, and perhaps the reporters who are reporting live from the scene of a story. The rest of the newsroom is hidden (but during a news broadcast, appears as chaotic as a battlefield).

Here's a glimpse of some of the things you don't see.

Hollering instructions into the earpiece of the stoic newsreader on the screen is an executive producer—one of the people who spend their days frantically trying to figure which news bulletin should go first, which should go last, and which should be scrapped entirely. Before that, of course, an entire team sifts through the massive volume of stories filtering into the newsroom, carefully sorting those that are relevant out of the rest. And that's not it. There is also the all-important technical team that ensures the uninterrupted broadcasting of news through the day. It takes extensive coordination between these, and many other faceless soldiers who work tirelessly to bring the news to you.

Despite the best of planning, however, there are always last-minute glitches that appear seemingly out of nowhere. 'If you're prone to panic attacks, this is not the profession for you,' warns Bhupendra Chaubey, a senior political reporter. His years of experience dealing with the chaos of a newsroom have taught him that things invariably go wrong at the nth hour. It takes a certain presence of mind and sleight of hand to salvage the situation before the news goes on air. 'Just the other day, a guest who was supposed to be live-linked to us from New York City got stuck in traffic and I had to change the rundown at the last minute. The viewer never knows what is happening behind the scenes,' he says.

NEWSROOM DEPARTMENTS AND THEIR ROLES

The newsroom of a television channel is somewhat like a complex machine that has several parts running simultaneously. For this machine to perform smoothly, even the smallest and most inconspicuous parts need to work efficiently. To make the analogy clearer, let's take a closer look at the various departments that keep the newsroom in running order.

The Input Desk

By the time a story is broadcast for public consumption, it has been thoroughly edited and perhaps even bolstered with a few solid facts. However, before getting this far, it has already moved between several departments. Nonetheless, the first stop is usually the input desk, where all stories are born.

The job of an input editor begins with extracting information from various news sources, such as reporters and stringers that may be based anywhere in the world. The material might come in the form of raw, unedited scripts or vague leads and tip-offs that may or may not prove to be newsworthy in the end. The input desk works with the forward planning desk (more on them below) to prepare a list of possible stories to follow up on.

Secondly, the input desk keeps on receiving data throughout the day, and then passes it on to reporters, correspondents and the output desk. An update on a cricket series will be forwarded to the sports desk and a story on a murder case to the crime desk.

Thirdly, when background information on a story is needed, it is the input desk that does the research. For instance, if a celebrity couple files for separation, their relationship history is researched by this desk. It's also the input desk's responsibility to keep the output desk up to date on fresh developments so that it can be added to the bulletin.

The Output Desk

Another important arm of a newsroom is the output desk. Their job takes off from where the input desk's role ends. If the input desk's job is to gather information, it is the output's responsibility to put it out there for viewers.

Firstly, once the important stories of the day have been culled, it's up to the output editors to ensure that they are put on air, complete with graphics, pictures and effects.

Secondly, an output editor manages the edits, does voice-overs and, if needed, covers important stories on their own. When the news is aired, the output editor sits in the production control room, working with the producers of each bulletin. If there are any doubts about the facts of a story, or more data needs to be gathered, it is their job to clarify details with the reporter. For example, if there is confusion about the number of victims of a train accident, the output editor is responsible for contacting the reporter who was assigned the job.

Thirdly, the output editor also has to change parts of the script in the bulletin. Normally, reporters are expected to script their own stories and then run them by the output editors. Sometimes, stories are picked up from wire agencies instead (Press Trust of India [PTI], Asian News International [ANI], among others). In these cases, all media outlets wind up with the exact same copy. In such a case, the output editor must re-edit the copy to create a script according to their channel's style and structure.

The Assignment Desk

A news story that breaks in the morning looks radically different by the time you watch it on the 9 p.m. bulletin. This is because there are usually fresh developments throughout the day, giving the story new dimensions. Although it is the reporter's job to track these developments, it is impossible for one person to learn of every small update. That is why a media house also needs an assignment desk.

Firstly, the assignment desk is responsible for keeping a tab on the day-to-day and hour-to-hour happenings of every story. They also monitor the coverage on rival channels and alert reporters about developments they may have missed out on.

Secondly, in addition to assigning stories to reporters, the assignment desk also follows up on whom the reporters plan on interviewing, and where they can go to cover a particular story. This section of the newsroom coordinates closely with the forward planning desk to draw up the next day's work plan.

The Forward Planning Desk

As the name suggests, the forward planning desk is the one that is tasked with thinking ahead. Their primary role is to list ideas that need to be worked on the next day by reporters or bureaus across the country.

Firstly, after the day's schedule is planned, this desk checks with the reporters to see that stories are being covered as assigned.

Secondly, the members of this team also watch other TV channels for fresh developments and story ideas. If they spot something, the input desk is notified and the reporter is asked to verify the facts.

Thirdly, all fresh footage from bureaus and news agencies is received here and put together for the output team. The forward planning desk has to ensure that each story is edited in time for the correct bulletin.

Bureaus

A bureau is made up of reporters that are based in a city other than the one in which the media house has its head office. For instance, NDTV has a head office in New Delhi and bureau offices in Kolkata, Lucknow, Ahmedabad, etc. A bureau is managed by senior editors and the senior management of the company. Depending on the strength of the staff at a bureau, they can be tasked with editing scripts and video footage as well.

Stringers

When it is difficult for bureau reporters and cameramen to immediately access a location, a stringer reports instead. He or she is a local resident who has a nose for news. When an event takes place, the stringer will take the photographs/ video, conduct a few interviews, and write a rough script which is sent across to the head office. The stringer, who is not a full-time employee of the organization, is free to send the material to various channels. This is why you often see the same footage on different networks.

The Production Team

This team is made up of a number of producers, each of whom performs a different function. The head of this team is a producer as well—the executive producer (EP).

Every EP usually has their own news programme or show, and they are known to nurture these programmes like babies. The EP directs shots, approves content, and ensures that the show is on track. An EP also deals with lost feed including missing video footage, technical issues, guests who don't turn up, and other such emergencies.

Secondly, there is also a senior producer who shares responsibilities with the EP. Researching stories, writing them up, and selecting video to go with the stories are some of the areas these two producers work on together.

Thirdly, producers and assistant producers help write shows and perform related tasks such as confirming the guests on a debate or getting props for a show.

The Guest Coordination Desk

What would a news channel be without one of those heated prime-time debates? These days every channel has some version of them. It is obvious that viewers will be more drawn to the one with bigger heavyweights on the panel. These prominent celebrities, politicians, artists, social activists are invited to the show by the guest coordination desk.

Firstly, the members of this desk are provided with a vast database of important numbers and contact information with the help of which they invite guest experts on a show. (This job seems easier than it really is.)

Secondly, the panellists of a show are not always located in the same city, in which case the guest coordination desk liaises with bureaus to patch them in.

Thirdly, every now and then a guest who agrees to come on the show drops out at the nth hour, leaving the desk with little time to convince a stand-in to fill their shoes. This is undoubtedly the biggest nightmare for the desk but nonetheless one that they have to deal with pretty often.

Graphics Team

These are the people who make broadcast news look good. From the names you see written below a reporter or anchor, to the grabs (photographs or video stills) on screen—the graphic designer plays an important role in bringing the news to an audience on a daily basis.

Firstly, when the news story being followed is about a series of events happening one after the other—such as, say, a natural disaster like a tsunami, or a terrorist attack—the graphic designers recreate the sequence of events on screen, helping viewers to visualize every detail.

Secondly, when people are being interviewed on a news show, the graphics producer types every guest's details into in a pre-designed phone placard. All the graphics have to be made ready before the bulletin airs so that they can be delivered while the anchor is at work or while the reporter is communicating with the anchor.

Thirdly, the busiest time for this team would certainly have to be election season. In a country like India which has as many as twenty-nine states and a multitude of political parties, breaking down votes and seat-sharing data in colourful pie charts and data sheets isn't an easy job.

Studio and Floor Managers

Before a show is taped, the studio in which it is being shot needs to be prepped. Floor managers or studio managers are the ones who set the stage for the show before it goes on air.

Firstly, they make sure that the lights are on and warm and the set is clear—extra chairs or furniture moved away.

Secondly, if there is a guest on the show, it is the floor manager's job to get him or her ready and connected to a microphone.

Thirdly, and most importantly, these members of the newsroom have to ensure that the cameras are at a proper distance from each other, with their heights adjusted according to the eye level of the anchor.

Outdoor Broadcast (OB) Van

In the early days of TV news in India, the entire broadcast was managed manually. Shoot teams went out with their cameras, brought in footage, and then the editing began. All the data was collated and prepped ahead of the news bulletin of the day. This was done well before airing time, leaving no scope for new additions.

Today we get news as it happens, in real time, and we have the outdoor broadcast (OB) van to thank for that. It operates outside the newsroom, but plays a significant part of the news process. An OB van is a mobile truck (often easily recognizable by the channel's logo painted on it). The vehicle functions as a mobile production control room and has equipment that sends footage to the office. This means that information is transmitted immediately to give updates and report live on TV.

QUICK RECAP

- The newsroom is always bustling with stories, news breaks and unexpected changes. If you find high-pressure situations challenging, this may not be the place for you.
- There is more to a newsroom than the anchor you see on screen.
- Two of the most crucial departments are the Input and Output Desks. The first gathers information while the latter puts it out.
- There other several other departments like the production team, forward planning desk, managers, etc. It takes extensive coordination amongst all of them to bring viewers the news bulletin on time.

EXPERT SPEAK: VAIBHAV VARMA

Vaibhav Varma is a consultant (news) at Rajya Sabha Television. He began his career in journalism with a newsreader contract at All India Radio and then proceeded to join Asian News International full-time.

Vaibhav Varma entered the TV media industry at a time when it was still growing in India. His only options at the time were Doordarshan and All India Radio. The 'big gun channels' as he puts it, were yet to take off.

The two major schools that offered media studies courses were the Indian Institute of Mass Communication and the Research Centre at Jamia Milia Islamia in New Delhi. Unfortunately, there were few seats for admission, so Varma was fortunate to get a casual newsreader contract with All India Radio while doing his MA in English Literature.

This experience later got him a job at Asian News International, the only TV media news agency at the time. Talking about his experience as a TV professional, Varma says, 'The starting point of news operations on any given day is the editorial meeting that looks at stories to be covered and how they are to be treated by our network. Of course, this is subject to change depending on fresh news breaks in the course of the day.'

He further explains how the coordination between the input and output desks binds the system together. The input desk gets all the news material and the output desk makes sure that everything is put together and displayed flawlessly. 'The initiative comes from both sides. The Input is in touch with on-field reporters and receives news from the ground and deputes them. It also follows up on incoming video footage, liaises with guests and experts for various shows,' he says.

Taking about the output desk, he says that it is their responsibility to process what's coming in—information, video footage, etc. The desk consists of the output editor, copy editors (news writers), video editors, production staff and anchors.

Firstly, the output editor decides on the headlines and stories to be carried in a particular bulletin. 'The news writer's job is to put together a read or a story package. He or she would do this in consultation with the reporter on the ground or with the research department. Secondly, the news writer might ask the reporter for a story package or a sound bite that he's looking for. So, everything is so closely dependent on the other. Teamwork is what works at every stage, and success or credit cannot be one person's alone, but of the entire team.'

2

Editors: Polishing the News

It wasn't until a major national crisis struck India in 1999 that senior journalist Sonia Singh truly understood the impact of television news in the country. An Indian Airlines flight, IC 814, was hijacked by Pakistani gunmen while in mid-air and forced to land in Kandahar, Afghanistan. After days of negotiation with the Indian government, the gunmen released the hostages in exchange for three Pakistani militants jailed in India. 'It's the first time I realized the power of television in influencing government decisions and the potential to misuse that power,' says Singh, who was an editor at NDTV at the time.

Earlier that year as well, when the two sparring nations were embattled in the Kargil war, the developments were closely covered by NDTV at the ground level. As an editor, Singh remembers having to take a couple of tricky calls on what information to broadcast and what to hold back. Given the sensitivity of the situation and that it was probably the first time a war was being reported live on Indian news channels, TV bosses had to make some tough editorial judgements. 'We had to make crucial calls every day on what should be aired, when, and how. The army was not used to how TV media worked and there were conflicting reports from the Pakistani side, so we had to be cautious, and learned many lessons,' recalls Singh.

The job of an editor may come with great power and influence, but there's a flip side to it as well. When things go wrong, or when big stories like the ones Singh has described suddenly break, the editor also becomes the fall guy. Whatever the mistake, big or small, the buck always stops with him. He can't afford to say 'I didn't know.'

In a newspaper, the editor has the final say on which stories will go to print. He decides if a story is important enough to make it to the front page of the paper or be tucked away inside. Similarly, the editor of a channel has the last word on all programming decisions. The decision to air the big, risky stories rests with him.

The first thing to note is that the output editor and the editor are two different people. Their responsibilities differ, based on the channel they work for. Nonetheless, they need to work hand in hand to ensure that a programme is going in the right direction. Coordination between these two heads is an absolute necessity.

To put it succinctly, the *output editor* is responsible for one edition of a programme. A shift of several hours usually has multiple output editors and each one is usually responsible for a specific show.

The *editor*, on the other hand, has to look into all editions of a programme. However, there may be cases where the output editor and the editor are the same person.

GOALS OF AN EDITOR

Firstly, every channel has a handful of regular programmes and each one has certain stand-out features that make it original and distinctive. A description of these features is called a programme remit. An editor must ensure that the shows don't deviate from this description. A programme remit may be formally written or verbally agreed upon amongst department heads.

Secondly, editors also have their own personal targets to ensure the success of the show. In fact, when an editor is interviewed for the job, he or she is likely to be asked to point out a show's plus points or suggest changes to improve ratings.

Thirdly, every show on a channel is allotted a specific budget that it has to work within. An editor must look into this as well. He can't afford to overstep the budget of the shows.

STAGES OF EDITING

Good editing gives life to a production. Careful selection of shots, their optimal arrangement, and timing are all factors that contribute to a tightly edited bulletin. The larger goal is to recreate an event through images for the viewers. The big challenge is to tell the entire story in just a minute or two. That's probably why footage needs to go through a series of editing stages before getting the all-clear.

Step 1

After the visuals are shot, the producer, director and video editor review the recordings. First, there is offline editing using copies of the original tapes. Usually, a time-coded copy of the original footage is used. This time code is sometimes called Society of Motion Picture and Television Engineers/European Broadcasting Union (SMPTE/EBU). To put it simply, this term refers to the eight digit number that identifies the exact hours, minutes and seconds and frames in a video. I know it sounds like quite a mouthful at the moment, but once acquainted with the workings of a newsroom, such jargon will become a part of your everyday vocabulary.

Step 2

Next is online editing. During this phase, sophisticated equipment is used to create the edited master or the final version of the tape. This is when sound effects, colour balancing and special effects are added. With the latest technology, high-quality, non-linear, digital editing is popular.

Non-linear editing allows the editor to make revisions easily without worrying about multiple versions. It allows direct access to a video frame in a digital video clip without having to watch the entire clip. Besides saving money, this also cuts down on post-production time as it allows editors to work on different parts of the production process simultaneously. With such advanced technology, Step 1, that is offline editing, becomes optional.

Step 3

In this stage, a picture editor comes up with innovative editing techniques to make the story more gripping. One such method is called cross-cutting. This involves the parallel editing of multiple events. Cross-cutting can be used to heighten interest by showing simultaneously occurring actions on the same screen. It can also provide conflict by editing two actions which will then come to a single climax.

To get through these three stages, one needs a fair amount of technical know-how, but even so, the primary skill required is a strong news sense. To be a good editor, be it in print or broadcast, one must know what information to keep, what to remove and how to gauge the short- and long-term implications of a story. For that, one has to be well informed about the background of a story as well of those of the main players in the story. One should also be able to identify the right people to interview.

As you can see, this is not a job that can be done in isolation. Hence, managerial skills are also crucial. In the end, being a team player and enabling people to work well despite a great deal of pressure produces the best results.

A TYPICAL WORKDAY

- After the edit meeting, the input desk assigns stories to reporters and tracks new developments throughout the day.
- The reporters work with the input desk or copy editors/script writers/output editors to file their stories.
- Copy editors later finalize package scripts. The scripts are voiced and then handed over to package producers.
- When ready, the package is handed over to an output editor or rundown editor to be placed in a particular bulletin. Typically, all stories are packaged by the evening prime-time bulletin.
- This entire process is subject to change. When a big news story breaks unexpectedly, everything changes, including reporter deployments, story lists and packages.

QUICK RECAP

- The editor of a channel has the last word on all programming decisions.
- The output editor and editor work together to make sure that a programme is going in the right direction in terms of content, budget and timeliness.
- A good editor should know what information to keep, what to remove and how to gauge the short- and long-term implications of a story.

3

Writing the News

Different kinds of writers exist in the world of television. There are scriptwriters who put words together to create reality shows, drama, telefilms and the like. Then there are also the writers who are responsible for writing lyrics of the songs that play before each entertainment show starts. And of course, you also have the news writers who script the news bulletins that you see (the anchor isn't really speaking off the cuff.) The voice-overs that you hear are also carefully written to have maximum impact on viewers. When every channel is broadcasting the same news, something has to make the stories on your channel stand out.

When on air, newsreaders don't have the option of repeating a sentence that was hard to follow. On the other hand, while going through a newspaper, a reader can go back to a line that was unclear or complicated. Since the anchor doesn't get second chances, the script of a news broadcast must be crisp, easy to understand and impactful—all at the same time. It takes a skilled news writer to ensure that the information is packaged well enough to be consumed in one go.

News writers, therefore, are in charge of writing news reports that will be read on air by the anchors and reporters.

While many broadcast reporters write their own stories, at larger stations they are aided by news writers. They add value to the script by performing background research, checking interview sources, and adapting inputs from wire agencies like Asian News International or Press Trust of India. Since news writing in broadcast and print journalism is not much different, it is fairly common to see writers transiting between the two mediums.

RULES OF WRITING

There are four elements of a news story—a hook, the context, the unfolding and the wrap. Generally speaking, the first couple of sentences are for the anchor to introduce the story and the last two to summarize it. The introduction should be followed by facts that back it up, preferably in the active voice. Words such as 'today', 'an' and 'the' are best avoided. Let's take a look at some basic pointers for scriptwriting.

Keep it Simple

This is the most basic and important rule of thumb for writing news scripts. When it comes to writing feature shows, the writer can afford to use flowery words for embellishment. A news story, on the other hand, needs to be simple, to the point and easily comprehendible by the general audience. Since somebody will be reading what the news writer pens, words that are tough to pronounce or have too many syllables should be avoided. Also, long-winded sentences are a strict no-no.

For example, let's examine the following sentence: *Friends and acquaintances believe that Tista was extremely possessive and had the tendency to isolate herself.* This could be written more simply as: *People who knew Tista say she was possessive and often isolated herself.*

Choose the Right Words

News writers have only a few words to tell an entire story. They must pick the right ones. The words should both sound good and paint an image for the viewer's mind (even though TV news has video footage as well). Here is an example of a story by National Broadcasting Company (NBC) News correspondent Steve Dotson. He uses effective imagery to describe a cave rescue story. Note that it not only paints a picture of the disaster but also tells us about the victim's ordeal.

Imagine slithering through a block of Swiss cheese a mile and a half long. Climbing up a thousand-foot maze dragging a broken leg. That's what it was like for Emily Mobley. She clawed her way beneath the earth for four days, after an 80-pound boulder slipped and crushed her in a cave.

Maintain a High Emotional Quotient (EQ)

Let's use the above example once again. The three sentences crafted by Dotson immediately evoke concern and sympathy for Emily Mobley. In this manner, broadcast writers need to keep a high emotional quotient in their script. They must keep in mind that they are catering to a large audience and that emotion is far more impactful than rationale.

Complement the Visuals

A TV news writer has to tell a story with the help of visuals. This means that a person or object needs to be identified the first time that he/she/it appears on-screen. The viewer must know what he is watching. Nonetheless, a script should supplement the visuals by giving additional information and not repeat what is obvious in the footage.

Keep the Style Friendly

The language has to be relatively formal and yet not stiff. Imagine how you would narrate a story to a friend. An easy style helps keep the viewers' attention.

DIFFERENT STROKES FOR DIFFERENT STORIES

News stories are either hard or soft and their writing styles differ accordingly. With hard news, you need to be objective, straightforward, to the point, and use the active voice. Writing soft news involves being creative, revealing a story gradually, and bringing in an element of emotion. Naomi Datta, an experienced entertainment journalist on TV, sums it up: 'A news script is factual, to the point and usually hard-hitting. An entertainment story is a news feature—and so is usually written in a more conversational, breezy style,' she says.

When it comes to stories on *science and technology,* the scripts need to read knowledgeably and feature in-depth research because this field is fact-specific. Technical details and full disclosure of information are necessary. Specific details, including the seemingly insignificant ones, need to be included. For example, if the story is about a solar eclipse, the script needs to explain what happens during an eclipse and not just say that it took place.

Sports scripting is similar to the previous category in that it cannot be written without comprehensive, in-depth knowledge. The scripts must be completely factual and full of information about what took place on the field. This means that a news writer or reporter who is covering a cricket match needs to know all about the game and its major players (not to mention its rules).

Political scripts are a part of hard news. They need to present at least two sides of the story—that of the politician/party it relates to, as well as the remarks of the opposition. Objectivity is important and so is the extensive use of quotes and sound bites.

Business scripting covers markets, government policies and industry. The writer has to be familiar with business jargon and use it both appropriately and fluidly. Facts, figures and graphical representations are often needed to bolster the script.

Scripting for *metro news* or news relating to a city needs a different approach. Details of the event including the 'who', 'what', 'when', 'why' and 'how' should be included. Piece to camera (PTC) from the locations is a must, along with long sound bites.

A SAMPLE SCRIPT

Jayeeta Ganguly, who has worked extensively in TV journalism, gives us an example of a script.

HEADLINE: FROM REEL TO REAL. . .A MONSTER IS IN THE CITY!

(PLACED ON THE GRAB SHOT JUST BEFORE THE STORY STARTS TO ROLL. IT IS EITHER SHOWN ON SCREEN OR RUNS ON THE SCREEN BEHIND THE ANCHOR)

Anchor (read out on-screen): This might seem like a scene straight from the reel world of Hollywood, but it is not. Today is truly one of those days when the saying that 'truth is stranger than fiction' is being proven right. . . by an adventurous monster that has taken the city by storm.

Voice-over (VO) I: This morning turned out to be 'not so joyous' for the citizens and administration of the City of Joy as they woke up to 'good morning' greetings from a giant MONSTER that decided to shake things up literally.

The monster was first sighted near the Maidan by a group of morning walkers. They say that it was first spotted behind the trees lining Red Road and then started advancing towards them. Initially, they thought that this was part of a movie promotion campaign, but their 'illusion' was shattered as the monster came nearer.

SHOTS TAKEN OF THE MONSTER [IF AVAILABLE] AND THAT OF THE DESTRUCTION TO BE SHOWN FOR ABOUT 30–35 SECONDS. THE SHOTS CAN BE 'LAID' ON THE LAST PART OF THE VO.

SOUND BITES FROM THE MORNING WALKERS

VO II: Right now, the city is gripped by panic and we request everyone to remain indoors. The monster has right now entered Park Street and although it has not destroyed any of our iconic restaurants, one does not know what it might do if it gets angry. The administration is doing its best to bring the giant creature under control. The air force and the army have been contacted and we have learned exclusively that the authorities have already appointed people who are watching the original movie in order to zero in on the solution.

SOUND BITES: PEOPLE IN ADMINISTRATION: POLICE, FIREFIGHTERS, WITNESSES

VO III Piece to camera: THE REPORTER WILL BE STANDING AGAINST THE BACKDROP OF DESTRUCTION: It is time for us to head home too, folks! We know that we are entrusted with the responsibility of bringing you the news, but we do not wish to be 'the news' as we could become food for a monster who did not give any thought before eating us. It's time to say over and out but not before wishing you a Happy April Fools' Day'!

QUICK RECAP

- Write your scripts in the active voice.
- Avoid words that are hard to pronounce for the anchor and difficult to comprehend by the viewer.
- Get to the point quickly. Find a way to get the maximum effect from the minimum number of words.
- Keep the tone of the script conversational.

4

NEWS DIRECTOR: THE JACK OF ALL TRADES

With so many different teams collaborating to bring the news to TV, it makes sense that somebody who is familiar with every department oversees newsroom activities. The news director is somebody who has to wear a number of different hats every day. He's the Mr Fix It, the experienced journalist who is also the manager.

If getting to this position is your goal, prepare yourself for a long climb. You can't start your career as a news director because the job involves a long journey up the newsroom ladder. A news director is like a skilled handyman who has the quick fix to every possible problem. He takes care of managerial issues, keeps track of finances, and on a bad day might have to fix broken equipment too.

Given all of the above, it is safe to say that the news director has to be a jack of all trades. He is in charge of a significant department, and has to make sure that the station's general manager is pleased with his performance. When it comes to educational backgrounds, the TV news director usually has a college degree in journalism or communications and maybe a postgraduate diploma in journalism as well. Nonetheless, the most required qualification for a TV news director is to have a comprehensive background in other newsroom jobs. Some news directors begin their careers as producers. Others join the field as reporters or videographers and work their way up.

THE JOB OF A NEWS DIRECTOR

Given the varied skill set expected of a news director, let's break down the multiple duties he juggles in a day.

Protecting the Channel against Lawsuits

A news director's primary job is to maintain the channel's journalistic integrity. This means that they have to be an expert in the entire process of content generation—from the early stages of getting a news story to vetting its authenticity, and then all the way to prepping it before it goes on air. For example, a celebrity can threaten a channel with legal action claiming that a news story is defamatory. Or perhaps a viewer can claim that the channel has recorded footage that invades his or her privacy. The news director has to guard the channel against all such charges. For this, a sound knowledge of media law (and of course, journalistic ethics) is a must.

Hiring and Mentoring Juniors

Keeping a track of résumés, hiring staff and looking into their needs are some of the news director's managerial duties. Besides, they are also tasked with being a 'coach' to the rest of the team. Junior-level team members will look to them for constant on-the-job training, and so the news director must also be a suitable role model.

Decoding the Target Audience

Branding is another area in which the news director has to excel. In a competitive environment with so many channels, this job doesn't end with a show being aired. The news director must also ensure that the show is reaching the right audience. Channels usually conduct market research to understand who are watching their shows, what the viewers like and what they don't. The news director must keep in touch with the results of these studies and use them to better the channel's performance.

Keeping the Ratings High

'Target Rating Points' (or TRP) is a phrase one hears a great deal in the newsroom. To put it simply, it is this number that tells you how popular your show is and how it fares in comparison with shows on rival channels. I'm sure you've seen hoardings and ads where anchors boast about theirs being the most watched channel. Well, you can blame TRPs for their arrogance! For the most part, however, these numbers are a source of constant stress, especially for the news director. If a show's ratings are dipping, the news director needs to find out why, and fix it. Conversely, if a show is making the audience happy, the news director needs to pinpoint the winning formula and employ it in other situations.

With a duty list this long, it's obvious that time management is a talent that the news director must possess. They could be tasked with sitting in on a department meeting discussing budgets, responding to breaking news by dispatching journalists to the scene, and getting an anchor on air for the current bulletin—all at the same time. Staying calm is the key.

There's no doubt that a news director enjoys some serious clout in the newsroom. But to say that they have the last word on all decisions would be misleading. There are others who play a significant part in making decisions.

Firstly, there is a TV consultant who influences how the show is run after market research has been conducted. This includes employing focus groups to identify the target audience.

Secondly, TV stations also have a general manager who oversees all the departments in the station. A minor example of their responsibilities: They get to decide if a new anchor desk can be bought based on the sales department's performance. Good sales, new desk. Bad sales, keep the old one.

Thirdly, the audience can also determine certain decisions. For instance, the news director may wish to get rid of an anchor who is always late and comes in to work drunk. But he also knows there would be a viewer backlash because the anchor is popular in the community. In this case the news director's hands may be tied.

There's no denying that the stress can get excessive at times. But it's not all bad. There are some great moments that make the long hours worth it. There is a feeling of pride when TV ratings are high and staff members win media awards. There is also the satisfaction of seeing people hired by you doing well as senior journalists. All this makes up for the hectic days.

A TYPICAL WORKDAY

- News directors usually start the day with editorial meetings where they oversee the news staff while story ideas are developed, select reporters for coverage, schedule stories for air, and slot time for interviewing, writing and editing. They serve as primary editors who ensure that news reports are produced in an effective, responsible and timely way.

- News directors are part of the news team and contribute content on a regular basis. In fact, they may also play the role of an anchor or produce various features or special programmes.
- When new members are being considered for the team, news directors are in charge of recruitment and hiring. They also manage the news department's budget.

QUICK RECAP

- News directors must be proficient in all the back-end work of a newsroom. They usually begin their careers as producers, reporters or videographers, and work their way up.
- The success of a show is measured by the Target Rating Points (TRPs). If these ratings dip, the news channel has a problem that the news director must fix.
- They act as a mentor to the new hires of the newsroom. In fact, one of the highs of being a news director is watching protégés go on to becoming successful broadcast journalists.
- Despite the clout that news directors enjoy in the newsroom, there are still limits on what they can do. The opinions of the TV consultant and the general manager, besides audience perception, must be factored in to their decisions.

5

Producers: Building the Newscast

Imagine this: A few minutes before the show's broadcast is to begin, the reporter says that the person they were about to interview isn't turning up. What should the channel do? Should they go ahead with video footage and no interview, or should they replace the story entirely? Here's another scenario. It's a big news day—there's been a massive earthquake in Nepal, and at the same time, Rahul Gandhi has found himself in the middle of yet another controversy. Which story should one give priority to?

The answer to these problems lies with the news producer. It is their job to find quick solutions—sometimes within minutes—to ensure an uninterrupted flow of news. As viewers, most people take the smooth transition between programmes, news updates, and commercial segments for granted. When you're on the other side of the action, you'll see that this seamless presentation doesn't happen by itself. It is the producers who are responsible for integrating a station's varied content. They coordinate the schedules of various departments, such as news, programming, and advertising, as well as assigning work to announcers, writers and other producers.

A good producer should have enough of an ego to make important decisions and defend them, but they should not be averse to drudge work either. Writing a script last minute may even be a part of the job. Most producers rise in the ranks from positions of production assistant, so they know what it takes to get a show up and running—from concept to broadcast. They ultimately get credit for a successful broadcast but also have to take the blame for anything that goes wrong. If a big news item is missed in the evening broadcast or the video footage accompanying a story does not offer a clear picture of the news, the producer is answerable.

CONFLICTS IN PLANNING A RUNDOWN

Ranveer Singh, a broadcast journalist with ABP News, says the most crucial responsibility of a producer is making sure that no news is missed, or broadcast wrongly. 'That means that even a subordinate's mistake can be costly,' he says. He believes that a successful producer must have good research skills (keeping track of news in print and online), must be able to recognize the value of news, and also to learn how to predict the fallout of a story and prepare for the consequences accordingly.

Planning a rundown is a job which requires the producer to exercise their news sense. Regional channels generally start their rundown with the most popular local story. Then they follow with major news stories from around the country, and finally, around the globe. Taking Bengali channels as an example, if there are elections taking place in the state, that will be the first item covered. That will be followed by other local news, perhaps related to crime and maybe the results of a local football game.

It's only after these stories have been dealt with that the show moves to national stories—say, perhaps the prime minister's visit to a foreign country.

On the other hand, a national news channel with its headquarters in New Delhi will start with the prime minister and then go on to other news. Taking the example at the beginning of this chapter: Should the producer focus on Nepal's earthquake or on the latest controversy surrounding Rahul Gandhi? The producer could discuss the current trends with the news director, senior reporters and the production team to reach a decision. Unlike a newspaper which has set pages for sections like national, international and sports, TV news channels run on the producer's skill at news judgement.

A producer has to fit in at least five to six stories into a thirty-minute bulletin. So they need to focus sharply on which stories should make the cut, and among them what should go in the beginning and what should be pushed to the bottom. Another aspect to be considered is which stories deserve more air time and which ones can be addressed quickly. Therefore, a producer must have sound and unbiased editorial judgement.

There are cases where a producer may be influenced by other factors as well. Some news networks, for example, have political affiliations too. Therefore, their rundown may be determined by their political party's agenda. This means that certain news items might be intentionally avoided, while others could be given a great deal of airtime to boost a politician's image (for example, an act of generosity conveniently performed just before the elections). In these situations, the producer also has to find a way to balance their sense of morality against the pressure from their bosses.

STAGES OF PRODUCTION

Pre-production

This the most important phase, where the basic ideas and perspectives that guide the production are developed and set into motion.

Firstly, the producer has to clearly identify goals and the purposes of the production being planned. While doing this they must keep in mind the needs of the target audience—the viewers' interests, education levels and expectations. A producer might inadvertently end up insulting their audience members if they are too educated for a programme, or conversely, not educated enough to understand it.

Secondly, key talent is chosen and major elements like set design, lighting and audio are planned in this phase.

Thirdly, once a reporter has been commissioned to do a story, the producer prepares a storyboard for the treatment he wants to give the footage once it comes in. In the meanwhile, he may cull out other information about the story as well. Then he conceptualizes the graphics that will go along with the footage and ensure that he has the right graphic templates made.

After that, rehearsals need to be done before the actual shoot takes place. For example, if it is an on-location segment, the rehearsal would involve a quick check of everybody's positions (the reporter, the participants) so that as the camera moves, audio and lighting can be checked. Script changes can also be done at this point. This is the stage when production problems can be taken care of.

And then, the news producers supervise the editing of material in a section known as the edit bay. This area has VO booths where the producer has to make sure that clear voice-overs are recorded with no ruffling of papers or 'umms' and pauses. The producer is responsible for what goes on air.

When a reporter gives an idea, the producer discusses the treatment of the story—how it has to be shot and the elements it should have—with him. In the West, a producer always accompanies the reporter on the field. But in India, this happens only when it is a special story.

In the next phase of pre-production, the anchor and the producer receive completed scripts and the final list of news stories. The anchor goes through the script, marking pauses and checking the pronunciation of proper nouns. At this stage, the anchor can ask the news editor to change complicated words. If a sentence is not clear, the anchor has the opportunity to discuss this with the news editor as well. The producers make notes pertaining to the graphics, the duration, and exactly when instructions need to be given.

Finally, the running order (or the rundown), along with the final script is printed just before the show goes live.

Production

Once the news has been brought in from the field, the producer goes through the footage and sound bites, and then scripts the story. If anything is missing, the producer asks the reporter for further input. Once all the elements of the story are in, the producer has them edited; and when the story is ready, the producer does a final quality check before it is handed over to the output team that puts it on air. These are the duties of a story producer. Usually, each show has its own producer, although sometimes different editions of a show have different producers. For instance, the 6 p.m. and 10 p.m. hourly news segments will probably have different producers.

Production begins as soon as the footage is recorded. During the production phase, everything comes together for a final show. News shows are usually broadcast live while some feature shows may be recorded for later broadcast or distribution. In that case, there is a chance to stop the recording and redo things or make changes during the post-production stage.

Post-production

Jobs such as taking down the set, dismantling the packing equipment, handling financial aspects and evaluating the effect of a programme are part of this final stage of production. Post-production starts when all the footage has been captured. This is when the editing takes place. Producers make sure that everything from the script to footage is worked on to perfection.

ROLES IN PRODUCTION

There are quite a few members that make up a production team and their roles decide where they figure in the hierarchy of producers.

The *assistant producer* is at the entry level. They are usually given charge of getting on-screen graphics, such as tickers, ready for broadcast. (A ticker is the scrolling text running along the bottom of the screen, giving updates on news stories as well as upcoming shows on the channel.) A ticker producer needs to keep track of the smallest of developments and update the data constantly. In fact, whenever breaking news is shown on television, tickers help provide additional information to the viewers in places where audio cannot be heard.

The *rundown producer* is a part of the output team and decides the sequence of the stories that are put on air according to their relevance.

The *input producer* is the liaison between the story producer/output desk and the reporter on the ground.

Associate producers are involved in scripting and getting edits done. They ensure that the assistant producers deliver things on time.

The *senior producer* is responsible for conceptualizing ideas. This is a relatively senior role that also includes planning the flow of the show.

The *executive producer* is a managerial position. They are always stationed at the control room, running the show from behind the scenes. They are not only in charge of the technical personnel on the set but are usually also constantly shouting instructions into the on-air anchor's earphone. The EP takes decisions on what goes on air and is also responsible for setting budgets for the stories. It is the EP's responsibility to ensure that the story is delivered to the output on time. For this, they are assisted by the associate and assistant producers.

REQUIRED SKILL SETS

Strong Visual Sense

Angshuman Deb Barma, who has worked with Aaj Tak and NDTV, among other channels, says that a producer should have a feel for imagery. 'You need to know what will look good on air. You also need to understand the story and how to treat it. A producer cannot use every visual available to him,' he says.

For most news channels, it is an accepted principle that one is not supposed to show excessively graphic visuals such as the bodies of the victims of a bomb blast. One way of respecting this principle is by putting up an opaque patch on parts of the screen while reporting. Similarly, close shots of garbage or human waste are not advisable. Nonetheless, if the story requires such imagery—such as in, say, a story about municipal waste—the cameraman can establish that a place is dirty by taking a long shot of the area, and then following it up with a close shot of a person walking by with their nose and mouth covered with a handkerchief.

In 2004, Deb Barma covered the floods in Kaziranga where animals died in the deluge. 'There we didn't show any carcasses, but instead showed the water level and compared it with the average height of the rhinos, to show that they could not have survived under such water level,' he says. It is up to the producer to find a way out in these tricky situations and effectively convey the extent of the tragedy.

When it comes to feel-good stories, the producer has to ensure that a single shot is not repeated over and over again. For instance, while doing a story on Durga Puja in West Bengal, the producer must ensure that he is able to use not only the shots of Durga idols but also those of the devotees. While picking up shots of these devotees, he should be able to use extreme close-ups to get the maximum emotions out of these visuals.

Nose for News

How do you know if some event is worthy of being in the news? Most days the news production team receives more stories than they can use. A strong intuition in such matters helps, but there are also certain criteria that can help producers assess the worth of a piece of information.

First, a producer must consider the proximity of a story. If the event being described is in the present—rather than, say, a follow-up story for a past event, or a primer for an upcoming one—there is a much stronger case for the story actually being 'news'.

Secondly, the story's human interest quotient must be determined. If an event draws empathy from people, it is news. For example, a story about farmer suicides in an Indian state is bound to evoke sympathy. Or a hospital fire, for instance.

The third criterion is consequence—the social, political or economic impact that a story could have on viewers. Magnitude is another parameter to measure newsworthiness. Conflict is news. Sensational actions like ministers being caught in scandals are news.

Fourth, the entertainment value of a story must be considered as well. It's easy to feel a rush of adrenaline while watching a clip about a celebrity scandal like a brawl between superstars Salman Khan and Shah Rukh Khan—or even when the brawl ends and they hug and make up with each other at a party.

A producer has to constantly grade the stories that come in on a daily basis on all these counts. And they don't have all day to mull over it either; so it is crucial that they have the ability to identify a good story instantly. Bad judgement on their part could cause the channel to miss out on an important event.

A TYPICAL WORKDAY

- The producer begins their morning with reviewing the latest news updates. A review of the channel's broadcast is next in line, along with a review of any important mail that may have come in.
- Once in the office, they check the day's stories, including news assigned to reporters and other sources (such as stringers). They also monitor various other news channels and informational broadcasts as well.
- Next, the day's schedule is planned. This includes routine bulletins as well as special packages. The producer also selects relevant news from among the copy sent in by agencies (this includes video footage as well).
- Keeping in mind the requirements of sound and footage for the news stories of the day, they once again confirm and cross-check news. Sometimes, they personally upload it all on to a server online.
- The producer researches the content and background of stories to make sure that news reports are not missing any relevant details. Deciding the movement of the OB van and sending personnel out to report live on the news are their responsibilities as well.
- The producer collects necessary input from the input team, handing it over to the output team for the next broadcast. They also obtain input such as news coverage by the networks of neighbouring countries, and foreign input for international news.

- Ensuring deadlines are met for phone-ins/sound/footage/live data during bulletins and special programmes are a part of the producer's job as well. They also monitor tickers, make plans for the next day, including the assignment of stories/locations and specials. Their day only ends after they have assigned every last detail to the next team.

QUICK RECAP

- The three stages of production are pre-production, production, and post-production stages.
- Producers should have a good visual sense and a strong sense of intuition for what is newsworthy and what isn't.
- The newsroom has different producers collaborating on different tasks—for example, the rundown producer and the input producer.

6

A Reporter's Life: Finding the Right Stories

Reporters are the news-people who are hardly ever actually in the office. You'll most likely find them sweating it out on a bus to a remote location, or in the case of a busy news day, in the midst of a building fire, political riot or natural disaster—essentially, they go wherever the news takes them. It is their job to rough it out in the field in search of the scoop of the day.

There are some assignments that stretch for beyond a day, however, and reporters have to remain 'on-site' until they have ended. In 2012, when news of Shiv Sena chief Bal Thackeray's deteriorating health was announced, reporters camped outside his Mumbai home for nights on end till his death was officially announced. Veteran journalist T.S. Sudhir remembers doing the same in 1998 when former Andhra Pradesh chief minister Chandrababu Naidu took ten days to decide if he would give his support to the BJP. 'We journalists sat outside his residence, late into the night, every night, waiting to capture the moment on our cameras,' he recalls.

A typical day in the life of a TV news reporter begins the moment the morning newspapers arrive (and there's no telling when it will end). If you're planning a career as a reporter, make sure you're up for the commitment. To give you a preview of what an average day of a reporter looks like, here's a look at a fairly standard schedule.

First, after scanning through every available newspaper, a reporter starts making calls to sources or people who have stories to tell. Even if the reporter misses out on the 'breaking' part of breaking news, a good way to regain the initiative—and prevent being hauled up by the boss—is to get an exclusive follow-up story.

Second, as the day progresses, the story must begin to take shape. By late afternoon it should be sufficiently developed to be properly reported on. Prime time for television viewers is 6 p.m. to 10 p.m., so stories should ideally be ready before that.

Third, at the end of the day the reporter will be expected to check for updates on their stories and at the same time keep their ears to the ground for other news developments as well. As news comes in, data needs to be constantly updated. TV journalism is about visuals and immediacy. The more one adds in that department, the more impact a story will have. (Before retiring for the day, a final update is a must.)

Essentially, a reporter has to work at a breathless pace. Nonetheless, the biggest *pro* of being a reporter is that you have the thrill of getting to know what is happening before the rest of the world. You become a source of information for others and your work is noticed and read/watched by millions.

The *con* is that the hours are insane and you can be called into work at any point of time. But most importantly, the job of a reporter can make you vulnerable or put you in a life-

sometimes barely any time to gather one's thoughts, but even so, the reporter had better get their facts right. Mastering the perfect PTC is an art that every reporter learns over time, but if you keep these pointers in mind you should be good to go.

Firstly, for a perfect PTC, you need to stand still, in one spot—don't sway from side to side or move your feet this way and that. Fidgeting indicates nervousness.

Secondly, use hand movements to gesture to the scene or something that isn't within the shot; but be careful not to gesticulate so much that it becomes meaningless. If you have to move to show the viewer different parts of the scene, keep your eyes to the lens and have a clear path in mind before you start walking.

Thirdly, make sure that your background is relevant to the story. In other words, do not shoot in front of a wall.

Fourthly, understand that a PTC needs to contain important information that is central to the story. It should be clear why it is being included with the visuals and not as a part of the VO being read by the anchor.

A Reporter Is Never Off Duty

Do you remember actress Rani Mukerji portraying the role of a TV reporter in the film *No One Killed Jessica*? She'd take off at the dead of the night to follow up on a case she was investigating. The film was a fictionalized account of the real-life murder of New Delhi model Jessica Lall in 1999. The film may have taken a few creative liberties but it wasn't way off the mark in depicting the unpredictability of a reporter's life.

As a broadcast journalist you have to be ready to move at the drop of a hat. Your phone can never be switched off; you should have the drive and the ability to leave a meal or even deprive your body of sleep and rush to cover a story. Saurabh Gupta, who has been an NDTV reporter for five years, says, 'An aspiring reporter should know that what counts is passion. You have to be passionate to survive the conditions that you may be asked to report in.'

The urgency factor of broadcast media rules a reporter's life. For instance, when a story is unfolding, one has to be ready with their equipment to head to the spot with the camera-person. Facts have to be gathered from the relevant people, sound bites have to be taken, and the story must be put together. Make sure that you and your camera-person are in sync with regard to the angle of the story. If the story is developing, the reporter must stick around and be constantly on top of updates from the relevant authorities. Despite the fact that every other channel is scrambling for the same news, a reporter needs to be able to beat all the others to the 'breaking news'. A channel's TRP depends on it.

Unlike print journalists, who get a day to file fresh updates on a story, TV journalists do not have that luxury. Newspapers come out the next day, but TV news has to be updated every moment.

Another disadvantage for TV reporters is that important quotes from officials cannot be recorded over the phone, as it happens in print. Since broadcast is all about visibility, there has to be compelling imagery on the TV screen. Face-to-face interviews are crucial. For most people, the thought of jumping out of bed and rushing to cover an accident or blast may seem like too much of a sacrifice, but a TV reporter can't afford to grumble. In fact, passionate reporters usually feed off the rush of being called to duty at odd hours and performing under pressure situations.

Cultivate Influential Sources

The infamous Watergate scandal of 1972 that brought down the Richard Nixon administration in the United States of America is still the most relevant example of why a reporter should not only cultivate sources but also protect them. *Washington Post* reporters Bob Woodward and Carl Bernstein brought down an entire government with the help of tip-offs from a government official whom they called 'Deep Throat'. The reporters documented the entire episode in the book *All the President's Men*, which was later turned into an Oscar-winning movie. But the true identity of 'Deep Throat' was only revealed in 2005, thirty-one years after Nixon's resignation. The mysterious whistle-blower turned out to be Mark Felt, the former associate director of the Federal Bureau of Investigation (FBI).

Another lesson here for reporters is that if you want to go beyond the surface of a story, to dig deeper into the workings of a company or party, you need to make friends with people inside the system. This is what is called cultivating sources. These sources are not official spokespersons—they could just as easily be a highly placed individual as they could be an inconspicuous person within an organization. Despite the fact that they may not be able to openly be interviewed on, sources of these kinds can definitely tell you where to look for your story.

Sources can't be developed overnight. Once a reporter has a specific beat, they need to identify important people in the area and set up meetings with them, to keep in touch with them regularly and build a strong rapport. Don't be surprised if you start spending more hours a day with your sources than friends and family!

A reporter shares a need-based relationship with sources. Sources offer valuable information, tip-offs on big announcements, and sometimes classified data. There are times when a source puts his own job on the line to sneak data to a reporter. Naturally, there has to be an element of trust in the relationship. Always remember to protect the identity of your source.

Vet PR-driven Stories

When it comes to big stories, such as an important announcement by a corporate entity, political party or a celebrity, you'll most likely be served the news on a platter. Organizations of these kinds have efficient public relations machinery to keep media house up to date on major developments. 'You need to have the right sources in the party office or be on a direct line with the minister's PA. It is prudent to be on the phone with your sources all the time. You should never throw away or misplace a number. And always remember to respect your sources for giving you inputs and being accessible to you,' says Jayeeta Ganguly, who has had extensive experience in both print and broadcast journalism.

PR professionals are your gateway to the people who matter. This is especially relevant for an entertainment reporter. Before the release of a film, the PR team arranges interactions with the actors to help generate hype about the movie. After the movie releases, the PR team may send you data as proof of the film's success. The reporter must carefully vet all the communication sent to them by a public figure's PR machinery. Do not take everything they tell you at face value. While you must be on good terms with a PR manager, it is equally important to objectively view the information they provide and to cross-check all the facts.

Track Newspapers and Social Media

Over the years, Charul Malik, an award-winning journalist, has learnt that a reporter must keep in touch with the news at all times—even on holidays and days off. 'Once I returned from a holiday of a week and my boss remarked, "You are looking blank." Then we both realized it was because I had not read a newspaper or watched the news during that time. If an anchor is clueless, his/her face immediately gives it away,' she says.

Reporters need to pitch story ideas on a regular basis. You can do that only if you keep an eye on trends through the social media, contacts and general alertness. Sometimes stories just arrive of their own accord, but more often than not, a reporter needs to go hunting for one.

A broadcast reporter often gets their ideas from a newspaper or from the Internet. Every medium feeds off the others. What is trending online can become the broadcast of the day too. Keen observation powers and an institutional memory are also excellent means of getting fresh story ideas to draw in viewers. For instance, during actor Sanjay Dutt's trial for the 1993 bomb blasts, there was a lot of footage of him coming in and out of court. But only one reporter observed that the actor always wore a blue shirt to court. It turned out that blue was his lucky colour. The reporter had provided a new angle to the story.

Plan Your Story

If you are going to do a feature story (political, social, entertainment or educational) or a documentary-style story, you will need to do a fair amount of planning. Work on the angle of the story first; that will help you figure out whom you have to interview and the shots that you will need. This is a time-consuming task that might end up taking many hours, so it is also important to keep the deadline in mind. In features, it is also advisable to work on the script first. Get a rough draft done on paper before going for the actual shoot.

Sometimes, a reporter could be covering hard stories—as Jayeeta did during the Gujarat earthquake in 2001—and still get the opportunity to do feature stories. The hard news stories were on the destruction and rehabilitation in Gujarat, but she also did feature stories on the Rann of Kutch, on the lives of BSF jawans who man India's border with Pakistan, and the lives of villagers of Mota Gaon–the village in Gujarat that lies closest to the border.

Never Pick Sides

Bias is an issue that always calls into question a reporter's integrity. A reporter should not weave their own views into a report. They should only be concerned with the facts and eyewitness accounts of what happened, how it happened, and when it happened. Unlike newspapers which have an op-ed page or editorial section for a journalist's own comments, TV has traditionally been all about facts. When a TV reporter distorts the presentation of facts to include his own values, he is accused of showing a bias. Still, the current trend shows that reporters and anchors are not as harshly judged as before when they openly take sides in a debate. Perhaps journalists are being acknowledged as humans with empathy and opinions just like their audience.

In some cases, a bias is justified. For example, the editor may choose to devote more airtime to the activities of the government than to local murders and robberies. The Opposition party may be unhappy about the government getting more coverage, but since the news affects the lives of a greater number of people, it is a justified decision.

However, in most cases, journalists receive a lot of flak for one-sided coverage. In August 2011, all the 24x7 news channels in Delhi were occupied with the coverage of Anna Hazare's fast. Every last detail of the fast was covered, beginning with the interviews with Anna himself to those with his supporters, like Kiran Bedi. Media experts opined that the television coverage was biased in favour of the then seventy-four-year-old activist. They argued that the media had taken an adulatory approach to the matter.

Bhaskar Rao, then director, Centre for Media Studies, opined that while TV was inherently a biased medium, the channels had overdone it in this case. He was quoted as saying, 'The main issue here is corruption, which is the elephant, but the media has given extensive publicity to "the elephant riders", which is Anna Hazare and his team.'

Well-known TV commentator Karan Thapar also admitted that the media was blindly siding with Hazare without representing the government's views. In a newspaper article, he was quoted as saying, 'They [TV channels] have been less than comprehensive in exploring the divisions or contradictions in Anna's side. They did not expose several of Anna's demands which may create serious constitutional problems.'

Another example of bias is the 2014 Lok Sabha elections that ended with Narendra Modi as prime minister. The election was probably more intensely televised than the previous ones. Every news network was throwing the spotlight on Modi and his life. There were debates about him too. Reporters shared the good, bad and ugly about him until it almost felt like the man was a born leader. The focus lasted for months and was compared to the long and detailed coverage of US president Barack Obama's campaign before his re-election.

At one point, Rajat Sharma, the owner and editor of India TV, said that the TRP of his news channel increased by more than 60 per cent when Modi was on the screen. In fact, Modi's interview with Sharma's India TV in April 2014 'garnered the highest number of eyeballs in the Indian news television genre', according to the channel's website.

While Modi has been praised for his communication skills and crowd-pulling speeches, the same hasn't been said about most other leaders. In other words, Modi is TRP-raising material. Then this kind of media bias is probably the reason that politicians like Mayawati aren't seen all over the news. Her large Dalit following can't increase TRPs, right? They aren't the target audience for major news channels.

A TYPICAL WORKDAY

- Start your day by reading all newspapers from cover to cover. At the same time keep a tab on what issues are trending on social media.
- Fix meetings with important sources to get potential story ideas. Your story of the day should be ready by 6 p.m., before the prime-time news slot.
- If a major story breaks, a reporter has to rush to the site to gather facts. Sometimes a story goes on for many days. In that case, the reporter can't leave the site till the assignment is complete.

QUICK RECAP

- Be a human being first and a reporter second. Show empathy but not sympathy. Keep your notebook and pen out of sight until after you look a person in the eye and introduce yourself.
- Listen. The best material comes from letting your source talk. Interaction doesn't mean that you rule the conversation.
- Briefly explain the angle of the story before the interview, including the time that it will be on air if possible.
- Get a phone number or email address to confirm facts. Never forget about fact checking. More contacts also means more candidates for sound bites and quotes.
- If you are not sure about something that an interviewee says, ask them to repeat it. You need to get it right.
- Reconfirm facts with research. For example, you could use the Internet to confirm organization details when a person uses the shorthand form to name it.
- Think visually when writing a story script. Try reading your script out loud to see how it sounds. Make sure it does not sound boring.
- Keep in touch with your sources because story ideas can come up, or follow-up story ideas for the stories you are currently working on.

7

Anchors: The Face of the Channel

In the early days of Doordarshan, anchors or newsreaders were hired to come into the newsroom at a particular time to read the news. They blindly read the script given to them by the desk, without any involvement in news production. With the introduction of news shows and the twenty-four-hour news format, this began to change. Today, no one is hired only to anchor a show. In fact, he or she is either a reporter or a producer who doubles up as the anchor. In most cases the editors anchor the flagship shows of the channels.

T. S. Sudhir, editor for south India at TV Today network, believes that one needs to slug it out on the field as a reporter before being promoted to an anchor. 'Coming into TV journalism for the glamour of it is wrong. It is a lot of hard work and a lot of sweat. It can get ugly and dirty. Lots of youngsters come in saying they want to be an anchor. You can't be a credible anchor until you dirty your hands in the field. You should be driven by news,' he says.

However, Rajiv Makhni, technology expert and host of NDTV's *Gadget Guru*, has a slightly different take. He feels it is okay to be driven by the stardom that TV brings you as long as it doesn't take away from your passion for the job. 'If somebody tells you not to get into this field for the glamour, don't listen. They are wrong!' he says. Makhni started out as a host for *Gadget Guru* at a time when news channels didn't have any dedicated shows on technology. Today, not only is he considered the last word on all things tech, he even hosts multiple other programmes on the channel. 'Even today, when I walk into a studio or live event, I have butterflies in my stomach. I'm still charged, excited and nervous.'

An anchor's job is coveted by many. Not only do new entrants aspire to the role, even people already working in the newsroom hope to get there. The reasons are obvious. For one, it appears to be a glamorous job because you get to be on TV. Unlike a print journalist, people on the streets recognize you and know you by name. Secondly, for young TV viewers, an anchor is the only visible face. The hard work of the rest of the staff remains unseen, and so naturally, being an anchor becomes the ultimate goal.

'Broadcast journalism may look easy and glamorous. There's the thrill of hair done up nicely, make-up and being watched by millions of people. But along with recognition and visibility, a person must give time and effort,' warns Shereen Bhan, who has been anchoring and producing shows on CNBC-TV18 for over a decade. 'The preparation that goes into putting a one-hour show on air is much more than the one hour you see. You need to have patience for this business,' she adds.

If you feel Bhan and Sudhir are overstating facts, think again. Or better still, take a close look at Sambit Pal's daily schedule as an anchor and reporter for Bengali news channel Star Ananda. Pal started his career with Zee News and then worked for Star Ananda and other major channels.

'For the morning show, I had to get up at 2:30 a.m., take a bath and get ready for office. I would leave my suburban home by 4 a.m. to be there on time. I used to sit with the night desk-in-charge and producer to see the stories being carried in the morning bulletin. Then I'd go through the anchor links the copy editors had written for me, make changes if necessary, and head to the make-up room. I had to enter the studio by 5:15 a.m. to start recording the anchor links for the 6 a.m. bulletin. I used to anchor till 9:30 a.m. and then go out for reporting work. My day was supposed to be over by 5 p.m. but sometimes I had to anchor the evening show as well,' he explains. This should tell you that the fame and glamour of being an anchor doesn't come easy.

BEING THE FACE OF THE CHANNEL

An anchor may be the face of the channel, but they are nonetheless backed by a team. Let's go over the work flow of a newsroom once again: A reporter gets a story, and informs the input desk, which in turn passes it on to the output desk. Then the flashes (news information shown at the bottom of the TV screen) are written, anchor links (what the anchor says) are scripted and the visuals are pulled out. From here on, the PCR is informed, and the bulletin producer takes charge of the news items and gives cues to the anchor. The anchor reads out the lines as the visuals are played out and asks relevant questions to the reporter over the phone or in a live chat. The producer guides the anchor through the entire programme by prompting them with additional information about a news item and questions to be asked. So essentially, the anchor is the face for all those people working behind the scenes.

That said, the anchor is not just a pretty face on television. As Sudhir mentioned earlier, an anchor has usually clocked in some years as a reporter. This ensures that they have a nuanced understanding of national and global affairs, making them qualified to ask the right questions on air and even to moderate debates on contentious issues. But to graduate from a reporter to an anchor, one also needs to be articulate, presentable and confident. Let's look at some of the skills that a budding reporter needs to work on.

Work on Body Language

The news is constantly being beamed to a million homes across the country, and so the person on the screen who is delivering it must leave a favourable impression on viewers. An anchor's body language and voice are two important features that can make or break a news show.

Firstly, nobody likes to see a newsreader constantly clear their throat or move their eyes around the room as though they are unsure of their words. Fidgety movements, such as repeatedly running one's fingers through one's hair is another sure way of putting off the viewer.

Secondly, gestures help lay emphasis on important points—a shake of the head, a clenched fist or a pointed a finger. But the key is to not overdo anything. Your movements should be small and subtle.

Thirdly, a confident anchor doesn't sit at the edge of his seat. Also, a slouching back indicates a laid-back approach. If you're low on energy or distracted, it will show on screen.

And finally, looks can be changed with make-up, but the presenter must have passion for news. To engage the audience, the news has to be read as though narrating a story to a friend. One also has to make sure that one's expressions are in sync with the nature of the story. You can't smile while reading out: 'Twenty-five children were killed today when a school bus met with an accident.'

Check the Sound

Some anchors sound different on camera. In that case, it is important to pay extra attention to pitch and voice modulation.

Firstly, it is very important for an anchor to note the tone and cadence of their own speech. That dictates how the viewer receives the news being transmitted. If an anchor doesn't pause at all, talking in an endless monotone instead, they will lose their audience.

Secondly, if words are pronounced incorrectly, both the anchor and the TV station look bad. (There are voice trainers to help anchors overcome such issues.)

Thirdly, you have to learn to rectify your mistakes. Pal says he knows a senior news anchor who used to watch reruns of his own show at the end of the day to make note of his mistakes.

Keep Your Cool

The job of an anchor comes with a fair amount of stress, but you can't afford to reveal any of that on air. You never know what kind of situation could arise—a guest may get offended by a question and walk out, or a heated debate might get out of hand. Even if an anchor is tempted to let loose and give their guests a piece of their mind, it is important to stay calm and carry on with the show.

Look Good for the Camera

At any given point of time, there are an endless number of important stories breaking around the world. There will be days when no matter how sleepy, hungry or tired you are, you will nonetheless be expected to put on a suit and get in front of the camera. The viewer must never know if an anchor hasn't had a good night's sleep or is overworked.

'I've often done a fourteen-hour day shoot schedule and then been asked to come back to work. And unlike any other job, you still have to look good, really good, as you are on a show being beamed to millions of houses. News is not our slave. News happens and you better be there to make sure you report it to the rest of the world,' says Makhni.

It's a great idea for anchors to hit the gym or practise yoga regularly. Not only will it help you blow off some steam, it also keeps you slim and fit for the camera. Earlier, one wouldn't normally associate glamour with journalists, but now it definitely helps to look good.

Back-end workers of a newsroom have no dress code and can afford to walk into work in casuals. Anchors, on the other hand, have to look presentable on air. They should not look vulgar or dull. The women need to put just the right amount of make-up—it can't be too bright and over the top, and not enough of it will make you look pale.

Though there are stylists for some channels, an anchor must know what they are comfortable with on screen. (Of course, some of them get a bit too comfortable. Next time you find yourself admiring an anchor's suit and tie, keep in my mind that he could well be wearing track pants or shorts below!)

Know Your Facts

If an anchor doesn't have their facts in place, they'll be found out immediately, and when you're on live television, there isn't much scope to correct your mistakes. It is important for an anchor to be thoroughly briefed on the different angles of a story before facing the camera.

Firstly, every anchor (this applies to reporters and producers as well) must read the morning newspapers from front to back, must regularly watch news channels, read news articles, and be active on social networking sites. They should regularly speak to reporters, and clear doubts regarding stories being reported on.

Secondly, an anchor can't blindly read the news. Giving perspective to breaking news will also be a part of your job. For example, one can't ask questions like 'What will be the judgment of the high court today?' No one can or should predict a judgment before it is delivered by a court of law, but once a judgment has been made the anchor must be able to explain the implications to viewers.

Thirdly, an anchor must have a sound general knowledge of facts relating to the news. For example, one should know the difference between a cabinet minister and a minister of state, or that the Communist Party of India (Marxist) (CPI-M) has got a decision-making body called 'politburo'. If you don't know a term, avoid making a fool of yourself by delving into those things on air. Instead, learn about them later, right after the show.

Don't forget that, a special show or a live chat show requires rigorous preparation. Take a popular show like *We the People* on NDTV which discusses the week's biggest story. To anchor a show like this, one needs to make sure that one understands every aspect of the topic being discussed. (There are nonetheless research teams that provide anchors in-depth information and cues for the questions to be asked.) These shows usually have a diverse panel of guests, so it is important for an anchor to be acquainted with their backgrounds. Moderating various views on a live show can be tricky.

Ask the Right Questions

There's a marked difference between an interview done for print and one for broadcast. In print, the writer has time for a slow build-up before beginning to discuss prickly issues with the interviewee. A TV anchor has to cut to the chase immediately. One of the challenges is to devise questions that produce compact answers because film can be edited to cut out portions but not compressed.

Firstly, as an interviewer, the anchor must constantly assess each answer he gets from the interviewee and shape their next question accordingly. You can't read out pre-written questions from a list.

Secondly, it is important to focus on a particular theme for an interview—broad questions will get long-winded answers that go off the topic.

Thirdly, stick to the role of journalist. An anchor cannot suddenly act as a debater, prosecutor or psychologist on the show. The anchor's job is to seek information for the audience.

Don't worry about embarrassing yourself in your initial days; many channels start fresh anchors off in early morning and late night slots which have a smaller audience than prime-time shows. This is where an anchor can afford to make their initial mistakes as chances are that they will go unnoticed. New anchors are often also put through mock tests where they are asked to anchor a show without the camera being turned on. As the saying goes, practice makes perfect!

QUICK RECAP

- An anchor is usually also a reporter, producer or editor of the channel.
- If you're in it for the fame and glamour, keep in mind that in-depth research, odd hours, deadline pressures also come with the turf.
- Television is a visual medium—so take care of your appearance, diction, voice modulation and body language.
- Interviewing and moderating debates is a crucial part of the job. Build a rapport with the interviewee, listen to every answer carefully and keep notes during the interview and close with a 'thank you' and appreciation.

8

Cameramen: The Stars behind the Lens

When one is reporting live from the site of an accident, riot or natural disaster, one is also playing with fire, quite literally. However, viewers tend to forget that the reporter is not the only one braving it out on the field. There's also a photographer present; and at times their job is even harder than that of the reporter.

Senior journalist Suhasini Haidar bears testament to this. Her long and illustrious career of reporting from danger zones has taught her that photojournalists often have it tougher than reporters. 'In conflicts, we must always remember that the maximum risk is taken not by journalists in front of the camera, but by the cameramen and women behind it. They don't have the benefit of 360-degree vision, as they see the world through a viewfinder,' she says.

At CNN-IBN, Haidar covered some amazing stories, like getting into Tripoli to cover Indian evacuations before the bombing of Libya. Here again, she credits her achievements to camera-person Nishat Hayat who went beyond the call of duty by filming round the clock in exhausting and frightening circumstances. In fact, Haider says she owes her entire career to the cameramen who accompanied her on stories. Margaret Moth, the late camera-person of CNN who was instrumental in making her a reporter, lived with terrible injuries sustained during a mortar attack that injured her jaw. Haidar's cameraman at CNN, Sanjiv Talreja, has covered everything with her, right from natural disasters and riots to violent elections. 'He would often have pains—a knee injury or a busted wrist—but one never doubted that he would be up and ready for work the next day,' she says.

There are several instances of events that have left a lasting impression on us through the photographs of what happened. For example, Mumbai's Taj Mahal Hotel burning on 26/11 as the sound of gunshots filled our ears; or the sea of humanity gathered at superstar Rajesh Khanna's funeral procession. These are images that stay with us. Without these images, the news might not have had the same impact that it did. The pictures and video footage brought us closer to the scene.

TV cameramen capture video images that enhance the news or features programmes. Some accompany reporters to the scene and others work in the studio. A video journalist is a multi-tasker. Their work doesn't end at capturing the footage. They also need to be familiar with the technology needed to upload their edited videos, complete with perfect lighting and sound.

The job typically involves working long hours because news happens round the clock. It can involve standing for long periods of time, working outdoors or in rough weather. But let this not deter you. Watching crucial news events unfold from behind the camera is a thrilling experience.

HOW TO LAND THE JOB

A news channel usually hires photographers based on the quality of their previous work. Before you approach a channel for work, make sure that you have certain basic things handy.

Firstly, employers usually ask applicants to submit a demo reel. The reel should contain the candidate's best work that showcases their skills of composition, visual communication, lighting, sound and video editing. This portfolio is the major part of the job application. You need to choose its content carefully. Do not use too much imagery or gimmicks. Choose a small number of examples that best show your range, visual storytelling skills and technical expertise.

Secondly, along with the DVD or link to your work, most news stations require their cameramen to have some experience. This experience can date back to high school projects. College degree programmes in journalism may offer internships where you can work for a local news station. Independent or contract projects are another way to gather experience before gaining full-time employment.

MUST-HAVE SKILLS OF A LENSMAN

Let's imagine you've got the job. You're now a cameraman at a leading news channel and are being sent on your first assignment. As you get to work, make sure to keep the following points in mind.

Think on Your Feet

The first step is to discuss the story in detail with the reporter and then visualize it in terms of pictures. A cameraman has to do this quickly, as and when news comes to him. In most cases, you won't have all day to plan the shoot.

Be a Planner

Ajay Sharma, New Delhi–based senior cameraman with ANI, has covered everything from earthquakes to wars to major political events. He says that a cameraman needs to plan well—and that includes considering the safety of your equipment. 'A good cameraman excels in his soft skills or personal qualities. If you are creative, have good visual skills, proper eye–hand coordination and can pay attention to detail, you have a better chance of succeeding in this occupation,' says Sharma.

Grasp Instructions Quickly

A cameraman is constantly being inundated with a barrage of instructions. Reporters, directors and producers will throw orders at you till the story is complete. Since you can't do everything alone, you'll have to pass some of the orders down to your assistants. Therefore, good communication skills and the ability to grasp what others are telling you are talents one needs to hone.

Master the Basic Tenets

There are certain basic rules of framing a shot that a young cameraman should master early on. First, the reporter should not be standing against a wall or a background that is irrelevant to the story. The reporter needs to be at the scene of the incident with elements of the news story in the frame. Second, a cameraman should not have the reporter in the centre of the frame. Having the reporter on one side is the best bet, because it makes them part of the action and rather than blocking it out.

Be Comfortable with Technology

A television camera operator works with digital, electronic and film cameras. They must specialize in one or all of the following areas: in the studio, outside broadcasts and on location. In the first scenario, the camera operator follows a camera script which details the order of shots. They have to interpret what the news director wants.

In case of outside broadcasts, the cameraman works as part of a team of operators who film live events (like a cricket match or a political rally). For on-location filming, the cameraman goes to the site of news. Here, there is more room to apply creativity when it comes to choosing shots.

Learn to Edit Your Own Footage

Whether in the safe confines of a studio or in the middle of a natural disaster, cameramen need to be quick on their feet and understand what makes attention-grabbing footage. They need to communicate with the reporter and anchor because most of what they shoot is live—that means it is broadcast without any editing. They also need to know the equipment used for video editing. You can't leave everything to the output desk.

SHOTS, ANGLES, CAMERA TRICKS, AND MORE...

Types of Cameras

Television journalism uses different types of cameras. These are the studio camera, the outside broadcast (OB) camera, the film camera, and the electronic news gathering (ENG), lightweight video camera. When the set is in the studio, as it is for debate and discussion programmes, it can be pre-planned. The people appearing before the camera can be placed with reasonable accuracy before the shoot begins. The camera operator can make sure that backgrounds do not clash and that the cameras are placed strategically, allowing them to cut from one speaker to another seamlessly.

In the earlier days, the OB camera would be as large as a studio camera and be mounted on a tower platform or the roof of a car. This created the disadvantage of limited mobility and allowed no control over lighting. The development of the hand-held camera and the directional microphone that can pick up speech at considerable distances has given modern TV journalists much more flexibility.

The introduction of the ENG camera was a boon to journalists because it could transmit pulses directly to the studio without any intermediary film processing. Before that, live events on TV were only those that could be planned beforehand (e.g., sports matches) so that the ENG camera could be set up accordingly.

Lenses

Cameras come equipped with various lenses. The telephoto lens makes a subject seem much closer than it really is. The wide-angle lens makes it easy to photograph a large group by making distances from the camera seem greater than they really are. Most modern studio cameras use zoom lenses which enable a cameraman to take a variety of shots without switching lenses.

Angles

A TV programme is a series of continuously changing images in which events are shown from a variety of viewpoints. The angle from which an event is shot can influence the way a viewer understands the story. A cameraman must therefore choose the camera angle that fits in with the kind of story they are filming. There are three basic types of camera angles based on the viewpoint:

First, there is the *objective camera angle* where the video is shot from a sideline viewpoint. The result is that the viewers can see the scene through the eyes of an unseen observer. This makes the visual somewhat impersonal. It is also called an audience point of view.

Second comes the *subjective camera angle*. In this case, the camera changes place with a person in the picture. The camera acts as the eyes of the audience by placing the audience right on the scene. When the camera shows a close-up of a person looking off-screen, and this shot is followed by subjective shots, the audience understands that it is seeing what the person on the screen is seeing too.

Third is the *point-of-view (p.o.v) camera angle*. This angle is used whenever it is necessary to involve the viewer more closely. It often follows off-the-shoulder shots—when two people face each other and are involved in dialogue.

Shots

While the size of the image is determined by the distance of the camera from the subject and the focal length of the lens, it can be altered by moving the subject or the camera or by using a zoom lens. Depending on these factors, there are different types of shots.

For instance, there is the *extreme long shot* (ELS) that focuses on a vast area from a great distance to show the entire setting or event. These shots are best when taken from a high vantage point such as the top of a building or from a helicopter. Then there is the *long shot* (LS) which covers the entire area of action and shows viewers the overall appearance of place, people and objects involved. A *medium shot* (MS) can be described as an intermediate shot because it falls between a long shot and a close-up. It covers the people above the knees or from just below the waist. This particular kind of shot is sometimes called the American shot because it was developed in Hollywood.

Full-screen close-ups of newspapers, photographs and other written material are called *inserts*. A *low shot* is one where the camera is angled upward at the subject, whereas a *high shot* is the opposite with the camera looking down at the subject. A *reverse shot* is a scene made from the reverse direction of a previous shot. A *reaction shot* is a silent shot that is a close-up of a person reacting to something that has been said. This could include a clapping audience or a specific audience member.

The camera's height plays a significant role in influencing the viewers' involvement and reaction to an incident as well. Objective shots should be framed from the eye level of an average person, but close-ups should be shot from the subject's eye level to have the viewer and the person on camera looking into each other's eyes. Point-of-view close-ups are recorded from the subject's eye level when the people on the scene are approximately of the same height, but from the opposing person's height there is a difference. Here are few examples of how a cameraman needs to adjust their shots according to the need of the story or event they are covering:

- Action occurring in depth, such as a field placing in a cricket match or a military formation, can be viewed in its entirety from a high angle.

- A level-angle or a low-angle shot can be used to record foreground action. By keeping a high angle, the camera can shoot across the entire area of action from front to back. In fact, high-angle shots enable you to keep a sharp focus across the whole picture area. They reduce the height of a person or object. In such a case, a tall person would look down at a shorter person in a point-of-view shot.
- A low-angle shot is one in which the camera is tilted upward to view the subject. Low angles can be used to inspire awe or create excitement by increasing a subject's height or speed. It can be used to eliminate background or to position persons or objects against the sky. Religious objects such as the idol inside a famous temple can be shot like this with the viewer in a lowly position, so that he looks up at the idol.

A TYPICAL WORKDAY

- A cameraman assembles, prepares and sets up equipment prior to filming, which includes tripods, monitors, lighting, cables and leads, and headphones.
- They plan the shots for a story and also advise the reporter on the visual impact created by them.
- They study the scripts to make sure that the footage corresponds with the news being covered.
- They keep up to date with filming techniques and equipment, and maintains equipment.
- Driving from location to location is a usual part of their job.
- After the assignment, they sit down with the editor to discuss visuals and editing.

QUICK RECAP

- The cameraman cannot work in isolation. They need to coordinate with reporters and other journalists to figure out what is important and what should be covered.
- Keeping in touch with filming techniques and understanding basic camera angles help.
- This isn't an indoor job unless you are a camera operator who films bulletins in the studio.

9

Finding the Beat That Makes You Tick

In the early days, a reporter will probably be asked to cover the entire gamut of news—petty crimes, civic issues and political developments. There may even be times when one feels frustrated about covering less-than-significant events that don't get much airtime. For example, senior political journalist Bhupendra Chaubey remembers his first-ever reporting assignment was a fire that had broken out in the Yamuna/Pushta area in New Delhi. He spent close to forty-five minutes talking to people who had lost their homes. 'When I returned to the studio, Sonia Singh, who was my boss at the time, asked if anybody had died. I said no. So she asked me to do a Voice Operation or Verified Transmission (VOVT) which shows a sequence of visuals while an anchor talks about them. No reporter is present,' he says. The story ran on only one bulletin and that too not a prime-time one.

Chaubey is currently consulting editor at CNN-IBN, but like him every reporter has to start small. With time, one graduates to 'beat reporter', which means that one is asked to report on developments in any one particular field. If you're exceptionally lucky, you may get to choose your beat. But that rarely happens. Your editor could ask you to report on a subject that he thinks you're cut out for, or sometimes you may be pushed into a beat that has a vacancy.

According to senior journalist Milind Khandekar, a good reporter can do equal justice to all beats. 'After all, it all comes down to spotting news,' he points out. Khandekar started his career in 1992 as a reporter with *Nav Bharat Times* and is today the managing editor of MCCS (Media Content & Communication Services). In his experience, if you want to specialize in a beat, don't expect it to happen overnight. 'If you wish to specialize in a particular subject, you have to start at the bottom of the ladder and climb your way up. For example, a political reporter may have to begin by covering a municipal beat or the state government before moving on to national political parties or the Prime Minister's Office,' he says.

A reporter's beat is not sacrosanct—at least not initially. If you're unhappy, you can move out and request for an area you're more comfortable in. Either way, your ultimate goal should be to pinpoint the particular area that truly interests you and then become an authority on it. This demands an intensive knowledge of a subject and building important contacts in the particular industry.

FIND YOUR BEAT

A budding reporter has many beats to choose from. Let's take a look at some of the traditional genres of reporting:

Legal Reporting

A law reporter covers various court cases and their trials. This requires a sound knowledge of the court's jurisdiction, its proceedings, hierarchy and legal jargon. The main news sources for a legal reporter are the law statutes, landmark judgments passed, court records and of course, lawyers. One needs to be able to analyse a case and give the audience the facts without using legalese. A journalist starting out in this beat must attend court proceedings regularly (and not just the high-profile cases). They usually begin by tracking smaller cases in the lower court, and then work their way up to covering the high court and the Supreme Court cases.

While reporting on court cases, all facts regarding the case must be accurate; the reporter can't voice random assumptions. For example, in 2008, when fourteen-year-old Aarushi Talwar and her domestic help Hemraj were found murdered in their Noida home, the Indian media was criticized for their unethical coverage. Some even called it a case of 'trial by media'. Before there were any conclusive reports on the investigation, the media had pointed fingers at Aarushi's parents, Rajesh and Nupur Talwar. Most of the reports suggested that they killed Aarushi after finding her in a compromising position with Hemraj, even though there was no evidence to support the claim.

In India, it is common for a case to be dragged for many years, sometimes decades. At any point of time, a reporter must have the case history at their fingertips. In case of the Aarushi murder, there were several twists and turns in the investigation and court orders that continued for years after the crime was committed. A legal reporter must add these to their memory bank.

Political Reporting

A political reporter usually follows either parliamentary proceedings or a particular political party. Parliamentary reporting includes covering the day-to-day proceedings of the parliament or state legislature. This involves tracking proceedings even with multiple party members arguing and speaking at once. A reporter must be informed on important bills and ordinances being passed in the House, and provide perspective on how they affect the common man.

A major part of this genre of reporting is the coverage of elections. Veteran journalist T.S. Sudhir remembers how in the initial days of twenty-four-hour TV news, NDTV had come up with the concept of following a politician from dawn till dusk in the days leading up to the elections. The idea was to profile politicians to get a sense of their campaigns and the work they were doing in their constituency before the polls.

The role of a political reporter is equally significant after the election. A good reporter will keep tabs on the performance of the government, check whether they have lived up to their promises, and watch out for cases of corruption and misappropriation of funds. In recent years there have been countless cases of politicians being embroiled in scams—the 2G scam, the coal scam, etc. All of these stories fall under the political reporter's ambit.

Business Reporting

This beat of reporting usually reaches out to a target audience—niche, educated and well versed in the economics of India and often, the world. The business reporter needs to profile business heads and interview chief executive officers (CEOs) of major firms. Talking to company spokespersons is a common part of the job. They need to know what major companies are doing every day—who is selling their company, who is buying a company, and which companies are merging.

The activities of the stock market need to be followed at all times. One can't miss either a rise or fall. For example, if there is a major event, such as the election of a new prime minister leading to major stock market rise, the reporter should be tracking it and know why it is happening.

Business reporters should have a strong hold on both qualitative and quantitative data because a part of their job is to have discussions with financial experts on national and company issues, including the budget. With specific channels dedicated to this genre, it isn't a surprise that many aspiring journalists choose to be business reporters.

Crime and Investigative Reporting

Gathering news on crime and reporting it involves the discreet selection of sources and maintaining a rapport with contacts in the police force. Sensitive information is often passed on to reporters in this field, so the identity of sources must be concealed. For example, there have been a string of heinous rape cases across the country over the past few years. While such incidents do need to be brought to public attention, there is a tendency amongst overzealous reporters to compromise the identity of the victim. In such cases, journalists end up doing more harm than good. Therefore, editors need to pay extra attention to the coverage of such sensitive issues.

Apart from contacts in the police, the witnesses at a crime scene are also important sources. Reporters will need to visit the scenes of crimes too, so you can't be squeamish about seeing dead bodies or blood.

Undercover reporting is an exciting but dangerous job. Reporters need to be smart about joining these missions because they can easily get caught in the web. In a shocking incident in 2011, Jyotirmoy Dey, crime reporter of a major Mumbai-based tabloid was shot to death in broad daylight on the city's streets. His assailants were reportedly members of one of Mumbai's notorious underworld gangs.

City Reporting

Journalists who report about a metro or city have to focus on local issues. For instance, a bandh or a taxi strike is a news story for city reporters. If a building in the city catches fire, that is their news story for the day. Every story is people-centric because the main audience consists of citizens from that area. City reporters need to remain in constant touch with their sources. They can range from a rickshawallah in a busy market area to a police officer.

Knowing the local language and keeping abreast of civic issues that the people care about is a must as well. For example, Bengali news channels sometimes show city reporters trying to catch cabs and then film the drivers' refusal. This kind of reporting can draw attention to issues affecting local residents of a city or region.

International Affairs Reporting

World news is brought to India by several international networks, but there are reporters in India who work in the field of international and diplomatic affairs. An example would be Prime Minister Narendra Modi's visit to Nepal in August 2014. Senior reporters, including Suhasini Haider, travelled to Nepal to cover the events of his visit. Coverage included an interview with Nepal's prime minister and other political stalwarts on the outcome of the visit.

These reporters need to stay up to date on what is happening around the globe at all times. They also need to maintain relations with international contacts such as government spokespersons. Even if a particular country is not in the news at the moment, one still needs to keep an eye on it so that no news is missed.

Sports Reporting

Writing and reporting about sports requires technical knowledge about the game. A reporter has to be conversant with the strategies, rules and scoring patterns of multiple games. When you're a senior reporter, you may get to specialize in covering a particular sport like badminton, tennis or cricket. Broadcast news also involves taking expert views on a match as soon as it is over. This includes a post-mortem of the team or individual's performance and an analysis of what they did right or wrong. Needless to say, this means you need to watch the match live, as it unfolds.

The initial years of sports reporting should be spent in building relationships with players and coaches. If you're covering cricket, you should not only cover the big-ticket international matches but also keep an eye on what's happening at the Ranji Cup level. You never know, the relationships you build there may pay off later.

Fans of a particular sport are not only interested on what happens on the field but also want to know about the lives of their players off the field. Recently, Indian batsman Virat Kohli's poor performance was blamed on his girlfriend actress Anushka Sharma.

Bollywood/Entertainment Reporting

Reporting on films or cinema includes gossip and entertainment. To get to actors, actresses and singers, reporters have to go through their publicists or the public relations managers, so building strong bonds with them is a crucial aspect of the job. They are also the people who could help in getting you an exclusive interview with a star way before the release of their film.

A journalist covering this beat needs to be social and alert for gossip. It implies that they need to have background knowledge about celebrities, their family lives, romantic lives, childhood and career paths. When there was a high-profile wedding like that of Abhishek Bachchan and Aishwarya Rai, the media dug out details on the guest list, menu and rituals. In the case of celebrity couple Suzanne and Hrithik Roshan's divorce, channels ran shows on the duo's romantic history, including how they got together and how long they dated for before getting married. There was also a fair amount of speculation on the reason behind the couple's split and a huge alimony paid to the wife.

Lifestyle Reporting

All news is not hard news. There is content that is similar to the features section of newspapers. Reporting on fashion, food, travel and beauty requires reporters to use a light note instead of the usual serious probing tone. For example, while covering major events like the Lakme Fashion Week, the reporter needs to know every detail about the designers participating, their creations and the names of top models.

Interviews have to be creatively designed so that they seem like interesting conversations and the graphics have to be appealing to the eye. The sound bite frames can be creative and not merely informative like they are in hard news bulletins. The visual effects are greater, and soothing music could be used. For example, during a cooking show, the ingredients are laid out nicely and soft music is played. The voice-overs for such lifestyle shows have a more relaxed pace than what hard news reporters get to do with their quick, crisp reports.

Health/Medical Reporting

Medical and health correspondents report on aspects of anatomical science, pharmaceuticals and the companies that make them, and hospitals. The discovery of a new cancer drug or an outbreak of Ebola virus would fall under the ambit of health reporting. Reporters on this beat must have a good knowledge of biology and the workings of the human body. Shows featuring health or medical topics often show graphics to explain what is being discussed. The reporter needs to know exactly what is happening when the image of a human body is shown—for example, the way a disease enters and affects it.

Important contacts for medical reporters are doctors, health ministry officials, physical trainers and nutritionists. The job can involve going on-site to where a disease has broken out and that requires caution such as wearing a protective mask. The 1994 plague outbreak in Gujarat was given massive media attention. The health and medical reporters shared the symptoms, the extent to which it had spread and precautions that needed to be taken. This also included shots of patients in various stages of the disease.

Weather Reporting

Regular weather updates are a feature of local news and form a regular part of a TV channel's schedule. Satellite images with detailed graphics that show weather maps are a usual feature of the weather bulletins. Thanks to graphics, the viewer goes flying over the country's map as temperatures are called out. A weather reporter needs to have good enunciation and look polished because their job is always on air.

Environment Reporting

When one specializes in the environment, one covers everything from rainforest deforestation and the extinction of species to debates about building hydroelectric power plants on rivers. Although these are all serious issues, the environment is considered to be a niche beat as opposed to politics, crime and sport. Having said that, there are examples of broadcast reporters like Bahar Dutt who have done commendable work in this beat. Dutt won the prestigious Ramnath Goenka Award for her investigation on the drainage of wetlands in east India that are home to a third of the world's population of sarus cranes.

While one shouldn't expect to get into their favourite beat on the first day, it is worth mentioning in your CV. If you've specialized in the beat during a journalism course, you may have an advantage.

QUICK RECAP

- Journalists can specialize in various genres of reporting. These include crime, environment, entertainment and many others.
- You rarely get to choose your own beat. Even when you do get one, you have to begin with the smaller

stories till you're experienced enough to be handed the plum assignments.

- In order to get into a beat, you should soak up all the exposure you get in the newsroom and beyond. That's the only way to become an expert in the subject of your choice.
- Once assigned a beat, build contacts with all the influential people of that area.

EXPERT SPEAK: MANISH BATAVIA

Manish Batavia has substantial experience in the broadcast of international cricket events and other big-ticket cricket properties. He has produced content for various magazine shows across sporting disciplines and has over a decade of combined experience in cricket and entertainment television, advertising and sports marketing. Currently, he is a presenter with STAR Sports. One of the shows he anchors is Star Power—Star Sports's flagship daily show.

Manish Batavia was working in the advertising industry when ESPN STAR Sports (ESS) announced the Close Up Dream Job—Harsha Ki Khoj—a talent hunt for a sports presenter in 2004–05. He had no formal media training but decided to give it a shot. He went as a walk-in contestant and did commentary for portions of a cricket match. The jury included cricketing legends Ravi Shastri, Wasim Akram and actress Perizaad Zorabian. He made it into the Top 32 and was booked for a flight to Bangladesh for live cricket commentary.

He got his passport just in time for the trip and found himself sitting in the commentary box with greats such as Sunil Gavaskar, Ravi Shastri, Wasim Akram and Alan Wilkins during an India–Bangladesh Test match. There was a public vote that kept Batavia in the competition. A studio round followed where he had to script, edit and present his own stories for the My Sportscenter round. 'I wasn't thinking news. I was just thinking sports,' says Batavia.

An interview and a promo-enacting round later, Batavia made it to the final six. Unfortunately, he didn't go further. But by then, he had developed a fascination for TV and knew it was what he wanted to do for a living. He joined a sports marketing company and spent five months there until Joy Bhattacharjya, the then head of programming at ESS emailed him. Bhattacharjya had given him his business card after the competition, saying, 'Keep disturbing me every week and remind me that I've promised to give you a job here.'

As promised, Batavia was hired as assistant producer and a presenter after a pilot episode he anchored for a wrestling show was approved. After close to a decade in sports and entertainment television, he understands the nitty-gritty of the field. During the years, he has been lucky enough to work with his broadcasting hero Harsha Bhogle.

His advice to aspiring sports journalists is something he was once told by Harsha Bhogle: Keep your eyes and ears open. 'Whatever I know is from working my back side off behind the scenes when no one was watching. I would spend hours in the edit suite watching video editors create magic out of raw footage. I wrote dummy scripts, re-voiced old scripts when there'd be no one in office, set up venues for shoots, and even booked equipment. I'd hang around looking at the little jobs that people on a TV crew did,' he says of his early days. Most importantly, he stresses on having fun at work. 'If you do, the viewer will too!'

10

Interviewing Like a Pro

A television interview is ideally a great conversation between the anchor and the interviewee. The job of an interviewer is to elicit candid and honest answers from his guests and get them to reveal their true personality. Television interviews have in the past turned out to be rather dramatic. There are numerous cases of celebrities making shocking revelations, breaking into tears or losing their temper on a show.

There's no telling which way a conversation could go, but the line of questioning depends on the tone of the show. Take BBC's long-running show *Hard Talk*. Personalities from all walks of life appear on the show knowing exactly what they've walked into. The questions are direct, hard-hitting and intimidating. If the guest has been embroiled in a scandal, he will be thoroughly grilled on the subject. When former Indian cricket captain Kapil Dev appeared on the show in 2000, he cried inconsolably when interviewer Karan Thapar confronted him about his alleged involvement in match-fixing.

A few months earlier, Dev had appeared on *Rendezvous with Simi Garewal*, a light, frothy chat show where he was asked a completely different set of questions. Garewal's show was more a celebration of his career, achievements and family life. These shows are non-confrontational, with an element of emotion.

Either way, it takes great skill to be the one asking the questions. Your guest could be a celebrated CEO, sportsman, politician or actor—you must know everything there is to know about him or her and tailor your questions to the mood of the show.

MUST-HAVE SKILLS FOR AN INTERVIEWER

If you see yourself hosting a talk show someday, you must start honing your interviewing skills early. A good place to start could be watching old episodes of your journalistic idols take on powerful people on their shows. Note the way they word their questions and how they handle their subjects—especially ones who are experts at dodging the question or who happened to be in a bad mood that day! Here are a few pointers that every interviewer must keep in mind.

Know Your Subject

The first and most important rule of interviewing is to be prepared. This means doing homework on your guest so that you can discuss everything that is relevant to his or her life. As you go through the information, questions will begin to form of their own accord. For example, if a celebrity you are going to interview owns a school for underprivileged children, you can ask them about that in addition to questions regarding their career. A senior journalist usually has a team to do thorough background research. Until then, don't be lazy about gathering information yourself.

If you are underprepared, it will show. Plus, the interviewee is always more receptive to a journalist who has their facts in place. A well-informed interviewer is able to shoot question after question at the guest, but conversationally, of course. Early on in Shereen Bhan's career at CNBC-TV18, she interviewed a minister from the NDA government about its disinvestment policy. The minister in question became acrimonious as Bhan cross-questioned him on the basis of the research she had done. 'It ended with him exclaiming: "Oh, so this girl will teach me now!"' she recalls. Bhan could deal with the situation because of her thorough preparation. 'Having the facts ready helps when somebody becomes belligerent. This episode helped me fine-tune my approach to my job,' she says.

So where does one do their research? The Internet is one easy option (for example, to access past interviews of the guest). But don't forget to scour other resources too like relevant magazines and books. Read every word of the article so that you understand the context in which they said things. Another way to understand your subjects is by talking to people who have closely interacted with them. Get them to share a few lesser-known facts with you.

Focus on Body Language

Conversation is not all about talking; keep an eye on your body language as well. If you're anxious, nervous or fidgety, it will immediately reflect. Make sure to keep eye contact, stay interested and maintain energy levels throughout the interview. Your guest will do likewise. Don't lose your pace, and remember to remain in tempo with your guest.

Be a Good Listener

To be a good interviewer, you need to ask the right questions. But your job doesn't end there. It is equally important to carefully listen to their answers as well. While your guest is sharing their thoughts and sometimes personal details of their lives, you need to be all ears—do not use that time to rummage through your notes to find the next question. A quick glance is acceptable, but anything more would qualify as being rude to your guest. Also, there is always the possibility of missing out on something important that has just been shared.

Be Polite

We are used to seeing politicians and supporters of various parties engage in loud arguments on live TV, with the anchor trying his best to butt in with his questions. The interviewee could be rude to you. Then what do you do? Nothing. You stay polite, ask your questions and stick to the agenda. For example, if you show a guest a document that proves that he has done something unlawful, he can go into denial and be verbally abusive. You can't react angrily or it will ruin your reputation with viewers. Keep your composure and let the facts do the talking.

A perfect example of how things could go horribly wrong in a heated debate would have to be a 2012 interview with West Bengal chief minister Mamata Banerjee on CNN-IBN. The show was an interactive interview involving a group of young students from her state. Faced with a couple of uncomfortable questions, the CM flared up at the accusations. She eventually stormed out of the event, but not before turning to the anchor Sagarika Ghose to say, 'You did not tell me before.'

Put Your Guest at Ease

Before you get going with your interview, make sure your guest is comfortable. If you put them at ease, there are more chances of them opening up to you. In a serious interview, you may need to throw some tough questions at your subject. Such shows can be started with the anchor announcing that the interview is about to begin so that the guest knows that he is on camera and cannot create any issues about that later. Softer interviews have a lighter and friendlier tone. Here you can begin by asking the guest how they are doing, or by complimenting their outfit.

A pre-interview is sometimes an option. If you meet the guest before the camera rolls, you can figure out what topics the person wants to talk about and what they want to avoid. Conversing before the real interview can help you get comfortable with each other. You could come up with new interview material if the guest mentions something that you didn't find during your research.

There are conflicting opinions on the merits of pre-interviewing. Some journalists believe meeting the subject before kills the spontaneity of the actual interview. There is always a fear of the final interview sounding stale because of repetition and loss of interest.

QUICK RECAP

- There are different kinds of interviews. They could be frothy and fun or serious and intimidating.

- Be a good listener. Carefully hear everything your subject has to say and cross-question them if something doesn't seem right.
- Avoid obsessing, and focus on the quotes that are important. You need to know how to differentiate between chatter and the gems.
- Be a little annoying and don't be afraid to press on topics that your respondent seems to be avoiding.
- That there may be some silences where you have to wait and let the person tell you more.

11

Routes into TV News

If you closely observe the résumés of senior editors running successful television networks today, one thing you will find in common is that none of them have had a formal education in journalism. Many of them began their careers during the days of Doordarshan and then graduated into becoming founding members of 24/7 television news in the country. Along the way, they learnt the ropes of broadcast journalism through hands-on experience. This explains why a few old-timers may argue even today that journalism cannot be taught in a newsroom.

Suhasini Haider, who was the foreign affairs editor at CNN-IBN for a decade, disagrees. She says today's generation of journalists cannot get away without a formal degree in the field. 'Today, studying journalism is a prerequisite for all journalism jobs. I think you learn many things only when you are thrown into the profession, but what you learn at a good school is important as it teaches you ethics and technique, and firms up the fundamentals of television broadcasting.'

Having said that, India didn't always have many options for students of journalism. The oldest surviving Department of Journalism in India was established at Punjab University in Lahore (now in Pakistan). After Partition, the department continued to function at the Indian part of the divided Punjab University until 1962. Now it offers a two-year integrated Master of Mass Communication programme. From 1947 to 1954, there were only five university departments of journalism. These included the University of Madras, the University of Calcutta, the University of Mysore, Nagpur University and Osmania University.

Finally in 1963, the Ford Foundation Mass Communication Study Team headed by Wilbur Schramm, who greatly influenced journalism education in the United States, recommended that the curriculum be made broader. This meant including the study of mass communication, advertising, public relations, and radio and television journalism. His report paved the way for a change in journalism education in India too. Along with that, it led to the creation of the Indian Institute of Mass Communication (IIMC) in New Delhi by the Ministry of Information and Broadcasting. Over time, the institute offered courses in each subject.

There are close to a hundred universities offering journalism and related courses in India now. Outside the university system, there are several institutes like the IIMC that offer courses in journalism. At the Asian College of Journalism, students can specialize in the television media stream. The institute has facilities to let students experience all stages of the news process, including production and post-production work. The course includes a focus on new media and the impact of digitalization on the newsroom. Top communication and journalism institutes in India and abroad offer diploma courses or degree programmes in broadcast journalism as well. Diploma programmes last for approximately one year and degree programmes can vary between one to three years.

The Film and Television Institute of India (FTTI) was the first institute to introduce courses in TV production. Its counterpart in Kolkata, the Satyajit Ray Film & Television Institute, offers programmes in television.

Here is a list of some of these educational institutes:

- Indian Institute of Journalism & New Media (Bangalore), http://iijnm.org/
- Asian College of Journalism (Chennai), http://www.asianmedia.org/
- Indian Institute of Mass Communication (New Delhi), http://www.iimc.nic.in/
- St Xavier's Institute of Communication (Mumbai), http://www.xaviercomm.org/
- Columbia University Graduate School of Journalism (United States), http://www.journalism.columbia.edu/
- University of Southern California School for Communication and Journalism (United States), http://annenberg.usc.edu/
- Boston University (United States), http://www.bu.edu/com
- The University of Sheffield (United Kingdom), http://www.sheffield.ac.uk/
- University of Westminster (United Kingdom), http://www.westminster.ac.uk/

HOW IMPORTANT IS A JOURNALISM DEGREE?

The importance of a journalism degree is a hotly debated topic. As mentioned in the beginning of this chapter, senior journalists in India all entered broadcast journalism through different routes. Sonia Singh, editorial director at NDTV, began working in Doordarshan after doing her graduation in English literature. Shereen Bhan, senior business journalist at CNBC-TV18, was all set to become a documentary film-maker when she got pulled into this world. And T.S. Sudhir, an editor at the TV Today network, moved to NDTV in 1995 after working in a production company, and hasn't looked back since.

Naturally, many of those who started out with Sudhir question the value of journalism courses. 'A formal education in journalism could help, but most youngsters armed with a degree who have worked with me have found it does not count for anything,' says Sudhir. He's also critical of the faculty provided by journalism schools. 'Most colleges do not have teachers with sufficient field experience. That to my mind is the biggest drawback in journalism colleges today. It is easy to sit there and critique, but being live in a hot and humid Chennai is not easy. What is needed is an aptitude for news and fire in the belly,' he argues.

Professor Mrinal Chatterjee of Indian Institute of Mass Communication, Dhenkanal, Odisha, feels differently. 'There are two reasons that a course in journalism is needed. One, the industry needs people who have an idea about the field. Two, once you study the subject, you are better equipped to handle it.' He also sees a prior background in print journalism as an advantage. 'Print journalism teaches you how to write. The entire thought process is structured then,' he explains. This aspect is important for any kind of journalism as it teaches you to collate all the information you get.

Ritu Singh, a senior correspondent at CNBC, also advocates doing a journalism course before entering the newsroom. 'Studying at Asian College of Journalism did actually help me prepare for the live TV newsroom. I knew the camera basics, could understand PCR functions, which added a lot of value.' She admits that knowing the background work that goes into production helped her get a better output. 'It does give you a feel of what it's going to be like,' Ritu explains. That said, she believes that J-schools cannot teach you how to be a journalist. 'It's something you pick up on the field. Television production technicalities help to some extent only.'

So it seems that attending journalism institutes is not a must, but mainly for value addition. For more on this, refer to the chapter titled 'Meet Your Idols' later in this book where senior journalists speak about how they entered the industry.

COURSE OPTIONS

Mass Communication Degree

This course covers all aspects of the industry, including public relations, advertising and journalism. Broadcast journalism will be one of many subjects covered in the course, so don't expect much hands-on training. It is an alternative route that some aspiring journalists take because mass communication courses are widely available. Also, they are often not sure about which aspect of the media they want to be a part of, and this course allows them to get a taste of all areas. Symbiosis University in Pune (and many local universities as well) offer a programme in this subject.

Broadcast Journalism Courses

A multitude of broadcast journalism and general journalism courses are available these days. In fact, most TV networks have their own training programmes. For instance, NDTV has an intensive training course for graduates. Whether you decide to study at an educational institute or at a programme such as NDTV's, you can get exposure to the field and secure internships, if not a full-time job at first.

Degrees on Other Subjects

Candidates who have degrees in other subjects such as political science, economics and English are often given the job of a journalist because of their writing and analytical skills. For example, if an economics graduate applies for the job of a business reporter, their educational background will be relevant. Or if a political science graduate wants to join political reporting, they will already know a lot about what is going on in that area. English graduates are known for their excellent written and communication skills.

Technical Courses

The cameramen, who are called video journalists, are a vital part of TV news. If you want to be one, you could study sound recording and TV engineering or video editing. Postgraduate certificates in these areas are offered at various institutes like the FTII in Pune. Start putting together a portfolio of your photography work, video clips and other relevant work. Try assisting a video journalist and see if that's what you want to do.

Distance Learning Courses

If you are working and cannot afford a full-time journalism course, there are distance learning options offered by Indira

Gandhi National Open University (http://www.ignou.ac.in), Sikkim Manipal Distance Learning (http://smude.edu.in), Punjab Technical University (http://dde.ptu.ac.in) and other institutes. While these programmes can teach you a lot about the theory of journalism, you won't have the advantage of hands-on training in a campus newsroom-like environment. There won't be the opportunity to work on video editing, production techniques or anything else that requires broadcast news equipment. This is why a distance learning programme won't really impress prospective employers in TV journalism. Still, if you want theoretical knowledge about how the media works, and absolutely cannot give time away from your job, go ahead.

PICKING THE RIGHT SCHOOL

If you decide to go through the J-school route, keep a few things in mind. Education is an investment. You need to gather as much information as you can before you spend your money and time on a course.

- Go on a campus tour or see if you can visit the department. Find out what kind of video production facilities they have.
- Do they have a special broadcast TV training room? Do students get to experience TV journalism in the practical sense or do they stick to theories in text books? Clear these doubts beforehand.
- Talk to alumni of the college if possible. Check if the campus has a well-stocked library. Journalism training involves lots of research and knowledge of various subjects, so you will need it.

- Last but not the least, inquire about their placement record. Have all their students been placed with organizations before they graduated? What kinds of organizations visit the campus?
- And don't forget to ask about internships. Are they a part of the curriculum? If yes, where have past students interned?

ALTERNATIVE ROUTES

There are thousands of aspiring broadcast journalists with degrees and diplomas that could earn them a job in the field, but not everybody gets in. Education is just one aspect of your CV.

Firstly, build a profile on the professional online network LinkedIn. You can browse through the profiles of channel heads and editors. Use the search box to type in designations such as 'editor' or 'bureau head' or 'anchor', and you will find all the key people you need to reach out to. Join groups for journalists. These are often used to advertise jobs and give out useful tips. Even internship offerings could be posted in groups.

Secondly, find people you know, even those you may not have spoken with for a while. Do this by importing email contacts or searching for names and narrowing results based on location, company, and other aspects. Look at whom your contacts are connected with because a lot of times you will know the same people that they know.

Thirdly, once you've got those established relationships, take them further by commenting intelligently on one of their home feed items or by sharing a story or article they might be interested in. Don't be pushy, but politely let them know you're thinking of them.

Fourthly, Facebook has a large number of professional networking groups too. These range from groups for job postings to those for general discussion. A few simple checks can help you separate the worthwhile groups from less useful ones: Does the group include thousands of members, or less than a hundred? How recent are the posts? Does comment threads fade quickly, or do discussions remain active? Does a variety of people contribute, or is it just the same people every time? Don't be discouraged if a group is marked 'closed' or 'private'. If the administrator accepts your request, you will get the chance to communicate with people you would never have met on your own.

Fifthly, find a mentor in the field. If this person is thriving in their career and has achieved success, they are a valuable person to have around for advice and contacts. Ask your friends, professors, and family members to introduce you to journalists or people they know in the media. Follow them on Twitter to see what is in the news and what they consider important. If you get an email address or phone number, find out if you can set up a time to meet them to discuss possible opportunities at the TV station.

Lastly, if you did an internship, keep in touch with the people there so that they can let you know if the station is hiring. TV news channels don't always advertise openings. Cold calling is normal in this industry.

As you can see, there is more than one way of making inroads into TV network. Unlike a corporate or banking job, where having an MBA degree gives you a definite edge over the others, a postgraduate degree in broadcast journalism is optional. If you have one, great. If you don't, no worries. You can always learn on the job.

QUICK RECAP

- Being a TV journalist does not require journalism study in your college or postgraduate years.
- A degree or diploma in journalism can be a plus point to help you succeed in the field.
- Universities and journalism institutes across India and the globe offer programmes in print, TV, radio and digital journalism. You have to do your research so that the investment is worth it.

12

GETTING THE JOB

It's been a long road of studying, researching options, and internships. You've applied to every channel you know. And then you get the call for an interview. What do you do? Start by immersing yourself into the channel's content. Keep your TV on and stay glued to the news and features shows.

If you know which show they want to interview you for, make sure you don't miss a single episode of it until the interview. It might help to take notes while doing this. What kind of tone is the anchor using? What kind of information is the reporter relaying during the PTCs? How have graphics been used to enhance the news? Are the journalists on the shows entirely objective? Or do they inject their own views? And yes, don't forget the names of the people you see on screen in case you want to cite them during your interview. For example, you could bring up the topic of an important debate that you saw and discuss how the anchor handled quarrelling participants.

WHAT TO EXPECT

Since it is your first job in the newsroom, you will most likely, be given a paper test before the interview. The test will differ depending on the position you're being considered for.

News Writer

You can expect exercises on writing scripts and pointing out problems in old scripts. You may also get a translation exercise because news agencies and stringers sometimes send in news in regional languages such as Hindi, Tamil or Bengali, depending on the location of the news story. If the prospective employers need a candidate who is bilingual, they will let you know before the test date is set.

News Editor

You will be asked to edit scripts or point out errors in them, including the description of footage to be used. You will be expected to correct the script, keeping in mind the time limit for a VO.

Reporter/Correspondent

Those applying for this role need to display their scriptwriting skills. They also need to know from what angle a news story should be covered. For instance, if you are asked about the coverage of a prominent building fire, should the reporter focus on the victims of the fire, or on the negligence of the government who owns the building? This is where prior research is important because some channels would point out the government's responsibility and some would not. A reporting test could also describe a news story scene and ask you about what camera shots should be taken.

Producer

If you are going to interview for a role in production, be ready for questions about the entire broadcast news process, because producers have to know it all. The test might have a list of news stories you will have to rank in order of importance. The objective is to know how good your nose for news is. For example, a regional Bengali TV news channel will most likely put a big Mamata Banerjee story as its main story for the bulletin and a Narendra Modi story later on. The national English channel will do the reverse because Modi is the prime minister of the entire nation. In fact, they may choose not to air the Mamata story at all during prime time. Observing the channel's newscasts before you head in for your interview is a good way to figure things out.

Cameraman

Aspiring cameramen have to be prepared with a disc of their work samples. This could include a documentary or footage taken at any event. Samples give the channel people an idea about your knowledge of angles, the zoom lens and shots. A fresher may not always be asked for samples, but having it ready can be a plus point when you apply.

Even with specialized roles for each person in the TV newsroom, some things are common across teams—knowledge of current news, research skills and writing skills. If you pass the written test and find yourself being interviewed, here are some standard questions to expect. These questions could be included in the written test.

1. Why do you wish to join this field? Is it because of the glamour or are you really passionate about news?
2. Tell us about your qualifications.
3. When did you decide to become a TV journalist?
4. Have you done any journalism internships?
5. If yes, which assignment was the toughest and why?
6. What interests you more—hard news, features or both?
7. Tell us about an assignment (while doing internship) that tested your patience.
8. Name some TV journalists that you admire and specify why.
9. Which news channels do you follow and why?
10. What news is ruling the air right now? Pick any two and share your viewpoints on those with us.
11. Do you think that news channels are biased? Why or why not?
12. We are giving you a situation: Script a story, mention the shot to be taken and do a PTC.
13. What do you think of the recently concluded General Elections?
14. How are you at handling stress?
15. What are your expectations from this field and from this organization?
16. Who would be the first three people to contact for a news story 'X'?

When it comes to the topic of your salary, sadly there isn't much room for negotiation with your employer. You should not expect to start with more than Rs 15,000 to 20,000 every month. The industry is not known for high salaries until you have several years of experience. Regional language stations will probably pay even less.

Here's a warning so that you aren't surprised later: Television news employees play multiple roles. This means that you could be hired as a reporter but would need to operate the camera sometimes. Or you could be employed as a news writer and be involved in research work along with scriptwriting. For those starting off in the production unit as a production assistant or trainee producer: don't complain if you find yourself dealing with tedious editing and camerawork too. Your employer could hire you both as an assistant producer and anchor. That would mean you would be in charge of an entire show in addition to being its presenter.

With advances in technology, the lines between newsroom roles have blurred. Think of that as a positive development because you will end up knowing how the entire process of news gathering, editing and production works.

IS AN INTERNSHIP NECESSARY?

The benefit of an internship is that it will show you how the newsroom works before you officially enter it. They may not let you do a lot, but even spending time observing others work is a learning experience. You could be sent to accompany reporters on assignments, be asked to edit a script, or even spend time in the PCR with the producers and news director to see what goes on inside.

An internship is something that you may be asked about at your first job interview. You can apply for internships at most TV stations by emailing them. You can also call them and ask if they're open to hiring interns. If you go to a journalism institute, they can link you up with an organization. Unfortunately, there are more aspiring TV journalists than TV news internships, but don't lose heart. Keep trying.

Some people end up interning for a newspaper instead. While print news is different from broadcast news, you can get the feel of the news if you spend time with it. You could even try to cover some events to see how reporters generally gather facts and put them together.

If you don't have an internship to talk about at your interview, be sure to mention other relevant work. This could be about writing for a school newspaper or about a documentary you made during college. Even extra-curricular activities in college (such as debates and public speaking) count.

For those who do manage to secure an internship: ask the editor and other staff you worked with if you can use them as professional references before you leave. After you leave, send thank you letters to the editors. Let them know that you appreciate the time and attention they gave you. It's professional and polite. The gesture could also help them remember you fondly when they get a call from a prospective employer checking your references. And who knows, if you're lucky, they may even choose to hire you in the future!

LOOK THE PART

Keep a smart casual outfit ready–a suit isn't necessary for a fresher. Men can wear polished trousers and a semi-formal shirt. Women can opt for a salwar kameez or trousers too. Whatever you wear, be comfortable in it. That includes your shoes too. Don't go wearing your highest heels or boots. Keep it casual but professional. Yes, that means that Crocs and flip-flops are not a part of the dress code either. If you wear nail polish, keep it to neutral tones like a light peach. Don't go there with red polish or red lipstick. And men, don't forget to shave.

Get enough sleep the night before the interview and keep copies of your CV ready to hand out during the interview because there could be more people questioning you in addition to the one you emailed it to.

QUICK RECAP

- Ensure you're well versed on the shows, anchors and content of the channel you're going to interview with.
- Highlight your strengths and weaknesses. If you have an internship on your resume, be sure to bring it up.
- You may be asked about your editorial opinion on the big story at the time. Make sure you have an answer ready.
- Speak clearly about your long-term goals in the industry. Let them know that you have a clear career path in mind.
- Have a list of questions ready to ask about the organization and job role.
- Don't arrive late to the interview. Dress appropriately. Don't act bored or uninterested. Keep your mobile device off.

13

Your First Days

Congratulations! You've got the job. It is most likely that you have joined as a trainee. So as the designation suggests—focus on getting trained well! The first day in a TV newsroom, no matter how big or small, can be overwhelming. The first thing to hit you will be the lack of order (when compared to most offices). There will be phones ringing, scanners scanning, printers printing, blaring television sets, and lots of stressed-out people talking at the same time. You can't wait for things to get less crazy because frankly, they won't. Just jump in.

Firstly, dress your part. If you are a reporter or anchor, wear suitable clothes for being on air. Keep a pair of jeans and sneakers ready in case they send you out somewhere. Imagine walking around a jungle area or the scene of a fire in dress shoes. Plus, you would feel odd standing there wearing a tie or suit. Wear colours that you look good in and avoid grey and white outfits—they make people look washed out. If you are a producer or editor, note what the others at the station wear. You could do that on the day you go in for your job interview. Women, don't slap on too much make-up. Use natural colours and accessorize minimally.

Secondly, keep notebooks and pens handy. A dictaphone is another useful tool for journalists. Nowadays reporters also rely on their smartphones to record conversations.

Thirdly, keep the business cards of all your contacts. Every contact is important because you could need them for your news stories. Your list should include numbers and contact details of the local police station, local hospitals, politician's offices and celebrities. Being new to a city is no excuse. Make an effort to know who is who and keep their coordinates handy.

Plus, don't expect hand holding in your first days there. The newsroom is a busy place. The trick is to be observant; look at what everybody is doing and absorb everything you've learnt. After you get acquainted with your computer, offer to write a VO or two and ask to look at some sample scripts. This way you can become familiar with the script formatting and style. If a senior seems too busy to give you guidance, understand that their schedule is hectic and push yourself to learn on the job.

THE FIRST ASSIGNMENT

Say you are a *cameraman* just starting your second week at the job. You have already shot some packages and VOs. You are familiar with the equipment but haven't faced a 'breaking news' situation. Suddenly, the assignment editor tells you that there has been a shooting at the nearby mall. 'Go right now,' he yells. You wonder about the instructions. What will you exactly do there, right?

At the site, there will be a lot of rumours; so more important than talking to bystanders is the need to get footage of the scene. For example, shots of the policemen at work or of survivors being escorted out of the mall. Later, you can take interviews with eyewitnesses and people who were in the mall.

While you are there, keep in constant touch with the producer and assignment editor so that they know what is going on. Don't forget to carry extra tapes and battery. Even if you have been sent alone, there will be a news writer or reporter at the station whom you will need to coordinate with. That means you must understand what's going on and have details from the scene too. You cannot just take some shots and come back with no story.

Now, say you are a *reporter*. You are being sent to cover a conference at the Press Club of India. Your job is to sit, listen, and take notes. What if you hear your boss get a call about a big fire in the city the moment you are supposed to go home? Don't go home. Think of relevant people to call and head to the spot to get a story. Accompany a senior reporter if one is being sent to cover the story. Learn the ropes as the news happens.

If you are a *producer, news writer or editor*, request copies of the station's newscasts. Pay attention to the stories, writing, delivery, live shots and the graphics that have been used. Watch all the newscasts your station offers. Early newscasts in the late afternoon are usually lighter in their approach when compared to the evening programmes. They typically begin with news and go on to features on entertainment or travel.

The evening-to-night newscasts are the signature newscasts for a channel. Find out the tone and treatment of these and the kind of stories that are broadcast at different times. Ask yourself questions such as: Does the station focus on 'live' shows? How do the programmes look? Can you do anything to improve them? If you have the answers to these before you go on the job, you will have an idea of how to craft things.

Producers, look into the sound and flow of the shows. That will give you an idea about the kind of writing style expected—something that you have to ensure is right each time. New reporters, notice if the reporters you see are throwing in their own views when they are on camera. Are they completely objective? Watching everybody can help you figure out how things work in that particular newsroom.

QUICK RECAP

- Dress like the rest of your new colleagues.
- Keep notebooks, camera, batteries and tapes handy.
- Don't expect to be spoon-fed by your seniors. Ask questions, keep your eyes and ears open, and observe the rest work.
- Find a mentor in the newsroom. Learn on the job.

14

MEET YOUR IDOLS

RAJIV MAKHNI

Popularly known as the Tech Guru of the country, Makhni is a technology journalist, analyst and television presenter. He was awarded the Anchor of the Year 2012 by the Indian Television Academy. Currently he is group managing editor, Technology, at NDTV, where he hosts an array of shows, including *Gadget Guru, Cell Guru, NewsNet 3.0, Walk the Tech Talk, Contrarian, Unboxed* and many others. He also hosts the international tech quiz show, *Croma Tech Grandmasters*. He is a multiple-award-winning columnist and writes on technology and gadgets for major publications, including the *Hindustan Times, GQ, Outlook, Mans World, Travel and Leisure International*, and many others. Makhni has been a successful ramp model in the past and is currently writing his first book.

BEGINNINGS IN PRINT JOURNALISM

The story of my journey into broadcast journalism is somewhere between a cliché and an overly romanticized Karan Johar movie. I was busy with a start-up business of my own when I got a call from a close friend who had just taken over as editor of India's first real men's magazine—not the sleazy and fun kinds, but a typical cars, fashion, gadgets and intellectual articles kind.

Since I was spending all my time and money on technology and cars, N. Radhakrishnan, editor of *Man's World* magazine, asked me if I could translate all that into a column. He was disappointed with the state of tech writing at the time and wanted me to write from the perspective of a user. He said, 'I'm only finding preachy people, those who think they are on a pedestal and can talk down to people.' Well, here was a chance to get my hands truly down and dirty with what I used to anyway do all day, every day.

My first column was a sensational hit. For the first time technology was being looked at without jargon, big words, and typically nerd talk. This was opinionated, personal and from the heart. Within a month, I was also writing for the *Hindustan Times*, *Outlook* and *Outlook Traveller*.

FIRST TV AUDITION

A few months later, I received a call from NDTV. They had launched a new show called *Gadget Guru* and wanted me to come on board as an expert. I was told that I had to talk with the anchor of the show, Vikram Chandra. I went with a lot of expectations because NDTV, in my mind, was this iconic media house that had given birth to news broadcast in the country. I had this entire scenario built up in my head where I would walk into an ultra-swanky, hi-tech set that looked straight out of a *Star Wars* movie. I imagined there would be 60–70 people in production milling around and some serious rules and regulations that I would have to adhere to.

When I got there, a young guy who looked like he was still in school greeted me. I remember him being constantly busy on the phone. Instead of some swanky studio, the elevator took us to the NDTV office roof. It turned out that *Gadget Guru* was an experimental show, thus no real studio set had been created as yet. There was a sheet of thermocol with the letters *GG* carved into it that was lit up with garish red and blue light, and two iron girders used as seats for the anchor and the guest. I took all this in and waited to be briefed on my role, but the producer was still spouting venom on his phone.

Once Vikram Chandra came in, the camera started rolling. They hadn't told me anything about the flow of the show, my role as an expert guest, and whether I was to agree or disagree. I did exactly what I would do in my columns. My view was highly opinionated, strong and aggressive. Whatever Vikram said, I ended up contradicting; we were at each other's throats all through. Most people on the roof looked aghast at what had just happened. Finally, the producer ended his phone call too. He thanked me and said they would call me again but not before six months as guest experts could not be repeated so soon. I was pretty sure that it was because of the way I had been on the show. I mentally bid goodbye to NDTV and the *GG* show forever!

Surprisingly, I got a call from the producer the very next day. I remember thinking, 'How had six months passed so quickly!' In the few hours that I'd slept, the raw footage of the episode was called for and seen by all the top people who handled lifestyle programming at NDTV. They decided that I should be called back without being told that I was being considered as co-host of the show. They said they wanted me to do an extra segment where I'd have to answer questions from viewers. It was basically an audition in disguise and within fifteen days I was anchoring the show with Vikram Chandra. And to this day, Vikram and I are at each other's throats. It's called the highlight of the show!

CREATING TV'S FIRST TECH SHOW

While my entry into broadcast journalism seems like a dream, it wasn't all smooth. When Vikram and I started *Gadget Guru*, it was the first ever show of its kind. Today everybody has a phone, tablet and laptop, but in those days, gadgets weren't so commonplace and not as popular. Today everyone has an opinion on all things tech, but at the time it was considered to be niche. It was a struggle to get things right and even source products for the show. Most companies we spoke to were sceptical. 'Who will watch a technology show on TV?' they asked. It was more common for people to go and check out products at the store or read about them in typical tech magazines like *PC World*.

Content was another major issue. What was our target audience? Non-techies would say it was all going over their heads, while serious techies would dismiss it as pure fluff. Did we want to make this a 'show for all' and dumb it down, or did we want to take on tech at tech levels? I'm glad to say that we must have done something right as *Gadget Guru* went on to become a brand. Today you have a tech show on every TV channel in the country, but *Gadget Guru* continues to be the leader they all follow. It's because we got it right that we have seven tech shows on the NDTV network today. No other channel in the world has that many tech shows and each has a fantastic following.

Being a technology journalist, I face the challenge of dealing with a world where everything is instantaneous. Gratification is now, and must take place immediately. In this race for speed, there is a loss of deep thought and content that is well thought out. It's also a place where the chances of corruption are high. I may be chest-thumping a bit but there is a good chance that if a newly launched phone in India gets rave reviews from me, it may sell well. If I criticize it, it maybe the death knell for the product. Thus, for a company to get a great review and high praise on any of our tech shows is critical.

And yet the one thing that is unique and shocking is that till today, I have *NEVER* got a call from sales, marketing or Radhika Roy, Prannoy Roy or Vikram to ask me to review a product positively. This includes brands and companies that are the top advertisers on NDTV.

A WORD OF ADVICE

If you don't truly have the passion for the business, don't get into it. Every line of work is hard. But this may well be the toughest. You could do any course and come here, and you would still need to reboot, forget all you've learned and restart by learning on the job. Also, your daily life will be very different from anybody else's. In some ways it is similar to a doctor's life; you could come home after a long day in the office and then have to go back as soon as you get a call saying you are needed. The rule of the profession is that we cannot switch off our phones.

Never think of life with a single career vision. Get into broadcast journalism, but ten years down the line, when you've established yourself, think of what else you can do. I write columns, help start-ups, teach at schools and colleges, work on shows other than tech, do theatre, and race cars. It's sad that we are all taught in our formative years to think of one career. Life is multidimensional and comes to you from all directions. It's important that we make our work the same too.

T.S. SUDHIR

T.S. Sudhir is the editor for south India at TV Today network of the India Today Group. He's also in charge of the editorial requirements of Headlines Today and Aaj Tak news channels. Sudhir anchors the daily news show *Up South* on Headlines Today and documentaries over the weekend. He writes regularly for *India Today* magazine and the website. Previously, he's had a stint of over sixteen years with NDTV where he was resident editor (south India). He has covered every election in south India since 1996 and has a special interest in politics, Maoism, sports, movies and human interest stories. A Chevening scholar, Sudhir turned author in July 2012 with the biography of badminton player Saina Nehwal and in November 2012 was nominated by the Foreign Press Center of the US State Department to represent India in an exclusive group of journalists from twenty-five countries to cover the US presidential elections. Sudhir has also taught media and communication courses at several universities in India.

EARLY DAYS

My tryst with broadcast media started in November 1994 when I joined the Moving Picture Company which used to produce a weekly business show those days. I stayed with them for three months before joining NDTV as a business correspondent in February 1995. My next job was as a state correspondent for Andhra Pradesh.

Over the years, I worked up the ladder and by the time I quit in May 2011, I was resident editor (south India). I worked for over sixteen years in NDTV before I took a two-year sabbatical from television to indulge in writing. In June 2013, I got back to television as editor (South) for the TV Today network of *India Today*.

When I started out in 1994, and even in 1995 when I was with NDTV, there was little awareness of TV journalism because we were breaking away from the presentation of news patented by Doordarshan. For instance, during the 1998 elections we came up with the concept of following the leader which involved spending time with a politician from morning to night. The idea was not understood because the politicians were used to short interviews. In fact, in 1998, Chandrababu Naidu had a three-seater plane, so I could only put my cameraperson on board. There was no place for me. But in 1999, he remembered this and hired an eight-seater plane so that both of us could be accommodated.

TRICKY ASSIGNMENTS

One of the challenges of being a broadcast journalist is facing subtle and sophisticated threats. In 2009, when Ramalinga Raju of Satyam was exposed, I had an editor and a corporate office calling me to stop a particular aspect of the news from being broadcast. Corporations, politicians and police may put pressure on you to modify, drop, or carry a story according to their interests. You need to be firm. There is also the extreme pressure of breaking news because TV as a medium is a monster. It needs to be fed all the time. But care has to be taken to feed it the right stuff.

You must be truthful to the viewer even as people around you are attacking you for what you are saying. It happened most recently in Chennai when the AIADMK cadre was upset with even the most neutral analysis of Jayalalithaa going to jail. 'Call her goddess or Amma, not Jayalalithaa' was one of the more polite orders. Similarly, during the Hyderabad bomb blasts, there were mobs who didn't want me to report certain things, and then accused me of being anti-Muslim. The challenge is to handle such people while doing your job.

STAYING AHEAD OF COMPETITION

These days there are about twenty-five Telugu channels—a dozen or so channels each in Kerala, Karnataka and Tamil Nadu, competing with each other. And now there's also social media to contend with. Let me share an incident to describe how fierce the competition is. On 27 September 2014, it was Jayalalithaa's judgment day. We all knew that she was convicted for four years. An AIADMK lawyer told journalists that she had been granted bail. A major newspaper tweeted it immediately, relying on this source. But our channel wanted to be safe rather than sorry, so we waited.

On 7 October at the Karnataka High Court, most of the other channels except Headlines Today (my channel) flashed the incorrect news of Jayalalithaa being granted bail, based on the AIADMK lawyer's version. We continued waiting for our reporter who was sitting inside the courtroom. We were worried because the other channels had started flashing the news. Then, as soon as our reporter confirmed that the bail had been denied, we flashed the right news. We saved ourselves from getting egg on our face, while other channels did not know where to hide. The golden rule is to always cross-check with two sources.

Achieving accuracy in a report is extremely important. How to get the news first, check it fast, cross-check it with reliable sources and put it out there. All of this has to be done fast. And, of course, there are long hours. So a journalist in this field needs a lot of stamina.

A WORD OF ADVICE

You cannot be a TV journalist five days of the week, nine hours a day, and take two days off. It does not work that way. This is like a *junoon* where you have to be on top of the news seven days of the week, 365 days of the year. You need to read the newspaper every day. If news does not give you pleasure, you are in the wrong job. A nose for news and your ability to push to get news first and accurately count the most.

You need to constantly innovate. Learn the craft of understanding the language of the camera for storytelling. You will be writing to pictures, so learn to use the camera. Writing skills are also important. The right diction, modulation, voice throw and good attitude on camera, of course, help too.

And yes, team work is very important. You cannot work in isolation in this field. Everybody including the editors and cameraman help you get the news out there.

MILIND KHANDEKAR

Milind Khandekar is a product of the Times Centre for Media Studies and a recipient of the Rajendra Mathur Award for the best trainee in Hindi in 1991. He began his journalistic career as a sub-editor-cum-reporter with the *Navbharat Times* (1992–95). He started off as a reporter with Aaj Tak and advanced to becoming an executive producer. During his stint at Aaj Tak (1995–2004) he looked after the entire operations of the western bureau. With more than twenty-three years of experience, Khandekar is presently managing editor, Media Content & Communication Services (India) Pvt. Ltd (MCCS). From 2004 till date he has looked after the editorial content of ABP News, ABP Ananda and ABP Majha. He has authored a book called *Dalit Millionaires* which contains fifteen inspiring stories in Hindi and English.

EARLY DAYS

I started my career in 1992 with the *NavBharat Times*, a Hindi newspaper, as a cub reporter. Around that time, senior journalist S.P. Singh launched Aaj Tak and offered me a job. It was early days for television news in India. So I joined TV after three years in print. Back then, Aaj Tak was only a twenty-minute programme telecast on Doordarshan. As it evolved into a 24/7 channel, I too grew along with it. I set up the Mumbai bureau and eventually became the executive producer of the TV Today network.

When I started out, one of the biggest challenges was to convince bureaucrats and politicians to speak to reporters. They weren't as media-savvy as they are today. Fortunately, they are now well versed with the way the media works and supports their role in society. Another challenge was sending pictures in real time. These days we can transmit pictures by live view or the OB van, but that wasn't the case ten years ago. Earlier, the reporter would have to travel to the nearest station with connectivity. In 2001, when the earthquake hit Bhuj, there was no place from where reporters could send in their pictures. Broadcast journalists would travel all the way to the Ahmedabad office, delaying the story from going on air by a couple of hours.

SKILLS TO HONE

An important aspect of TV journalism is delivering the news in a short span of time. Limited information and the requirement for immediate action are a challenge that print journalists don't have to deal with. They get much more time to develop their story before it goes to print. A broadcast journalist doesn't have that luxury. When the Mumbai 26/11 attacks happened, the news had to be on air immediately. Such experiences have taught me that when information is limited, you must report only what you know and never beyond that. It is better to say you don't know rather than to give out the wrong information.

Often I'm asked about the skills one needs to make it as a successful broadcast journalist. I always say a keen interest in news is most important. Those starting out in the field should be curious about the world. You cannot be ashamed to ask questions, even at the cost of sounding silly. Someone might think you are asking a silly question, but that is still better than not asking due to shyness. By not asking questions, we run the risk of misreporting facts.

You must know the world around you. For instance, if you live in Kolkata, you should learn about every aspect of the city, right down to the sports and its prominent people. Know about the constitution of your country, read newspapers and watch the news.

Strong language skills are also important for a broadcast journalist. Whichever language you are working in, you should know it best. Articulation is the key to conveying the news correctly to viewers. If you doubt of your language skills, don't hesitate to take training.

Finally, be open to embracing technology. Television news has changed with the introduction of new technology and sometimes journalists forget that they need to work hand in hand with it. Their involvement can no longer be only on a creative level. Who knows how people will consume their news a few decades later? Tomorrow broadcasts may occur on tablets and phones. So you need to move with the times.

CHANGING TIMES

In the last decade, journalists entering the field have had to choose between two options—print or broadcast. Now, there is a third—the Web. A digital journalist is expected to have the combined skill sets of a print and broadcast journalist. They must know how to write good copy, take photos, make graphics and take videos to support their story. That said, a new-age reporter should first master the basic tenets of journalism and have a nose for news before worrying about the medium. Depending on the platform, only the presentation style will change, not the news. For example, if you are writing a story for a newspaper, the pictures are secondary. But when you do the same story for TV, words alone will not help; you need powerful images as well. On the Web, you need both. But in all cases, the story has to compelling.

A WORD OF ADVICE

The problem today is that most people enter the field to be an anchor or reporter. The basic aim is to be on air. But the truth is that the people you see on your TV screen form a mere 25 per cent of the newsroom. The remaining 75 per cent works behind the scenes. You have to look beyond the glamour and acknowledge their contribution.

Whether you go to a journalism school or not is of little significance. Formal training does no harm and can be a good way to start, but it all has to come from within you. As I've often said, I like to compare today's news to an Indian thali—a selection of different small dishes where you get a little bit of everything. Our audience is diversified and each person has a different taste. Of course, you won't have dessert as the main course, but at the end of the meal you won't be satisfied till you get at least a bite of something sweet.

BHUPENDRA CHAUBEY

Bhupendra Chaubey is amongst the most watched political journalists of his time. Having started his career with NDTV in 1999, he has come a long way in influencing and shaping public opinion. He started by covering local, city-specific issues which celebrated journalists don't like to focus on. But his ability to look for something more, even from a routine assignment, kept him ahead of his peers. At present Chaubey is a senior independent journalist. He hosts his own interview-based show on the channel. He was the lead anchor for his channel and hosted top shows on key days like elections. Chaubey has been awarded with several top industry awards and is a personality who commands a great deal of respect.

EARLY DAYS

I started off my broadcast journalism career with NDTV way back in 1998. Before joining them, I was doing my masters in film and television at the Xaviers Institute of Communication. I was actually gearing myself up to be a film-maker. In my school and college life I enjoyed going to inter-school debates. Public speaking was a hobby and I excelled at it.

When NDTV was looking for bilingual journalists, my wife, who was my classmate at the time, was asked to apply. She asked me to try my luck as well. So I made my CV and sent it over. A few months later, I got a call saying that Prannoy Roy wanted to meet me.

When I got the call, I was busy making ad films and also writing my own film script. Films excited me. My mind was made up on being in that industry. But then I went to Delhi to meet Prannoy Roy and his wife, Radhika, and it all started. They asked me to consider making a daily film—the news—instead of making a three-hour Bollywood film. I didn't know what the news was all about but they said to give myself six months and then I could go back to films if I wanted.

NDTV hired the Thomson Foundation to work with their new journalists. The well-known Ian Masters came and taught us the art of TV writing and how to think through a visual representation of a story. We learnt everything about TV journalism. Masters once said to us: 'What is the credibility of a TV journalist? It is next to the postman. You guys have no reputation. You just keep on delivering the news.'

I remember working with Ravish Kumar, who used to sift through the mail at NDTV and was being groomed to be a reporter. Those days in Delhi, the public transport was being converted to CNG. I was asked to accompany Ravish to cover the story. We were travelling in the same car with a cameraman when Ravish told me that I was making a big mistake joining this field. 'Look at the hours we work—from morning till so late,' he pointed out. I heard him with amusement. We went out there and I got a byline. It was exciting. Since I was good at public speaking, I got used to the format and style of reporting.

LEARNING FROM MISTAKES

A year or so later, there was a press conference and the BJP reporter was absent. Rajdeep Sardesai was the political editor at the time. He was very busy, in and out of the office, and we had never spoken to each other. But that day, he saw me and asked, 'If you are free, why don't you go cover this?' So I was assigned one of the senior-most cameramen, Narendra Gudawali. He used to work with Rajdeep, so he was familiar with where we had to go. He told me, 'Don't worry. We'll take you.'

I had no idea what was going on at the conference, but I took down points. When I returned to the office, I showed everybody what I had noted down. They asked me if I had asked any questions there. I said no. They laughed and said a journalist's job is to ask questions. They said to not worry and to do it next time, but I was embarrassed.

Even with that incident in the beginning, I think I have managed to succeed because of my approach and attitude. For example, even after that mistake at the conference, I bounced back afresh the next day, with the same energy. My ability to speak two languages (Hindi and English) has contributed to my success as well because I do the job of two individuals.

BREAKTHROUGH MOMENT

My biggest moment happened when I was asked to report on the wind chill. That happened when NDTV was a producer of content for Star News. There was a programme called *News Hour* which was anchored by both Arnab Goswami and Rajdeep. I was asked to do a live report bulletin for them.

I went to an area of homeless people in the New Delhi railway station. I started off with a piece asking the people how they were managing the chill. We took pictures and zoomed into the scene where beggars were sitting by fires they had lit. Soon, Rajdeep was indicating that I should finish. He was saying 'right' multiple times which meant I should end. So I did, and they moved on to some political story.

Interestingly, Radhika Roy saw the broadcast and thought my pictures and reporting was great. She called the output team and asked them to put the story back on air. I received a call asking me to go back to the spot. Then there was an eight-to-ten-minute piece on the show. Such a lengthy piece on a show hosted by Rajdeep and Arnab was an honour.

SKILLS TO HONE

I believe that there are certain skills that a broadcast journalist needs. The ability to articulate is most important. You may know everything about a subject, but you may not be able to talk about it with ease. You must also enjoy reading. Enjoy the nonsensical stuff as well as the stuff that makes sense.

Remember that on TV you have to be more brief and sharp than on print. Imagine making a 1,000-word editorial into a TV format. You must be quick, not stammer or use 'oohs' and 'aahs'.

When you start working you cannot choose a beat. Over time you should try to build domain knowledge in the area that interests you most. For instance, if you want to be a sports editor, you should know what makes each player special and how games are played. But in the long run, journalists should have the ability to critically appreciate everything, whether it is entertainment or sports or politics. Read five newspapers a day, including regional newspapers to keep abreast of developments in every location.

Be very patient, and have a thick skin. I call it crocodile skin. You may be the best journalist around, but your editor may not think so. Some viewers may love you while others may not. Don't be affected by all this. Just strive to be your best.

SONIA SINGH

Sonia Singh is the editorial director of NDTV. She currently hosts *The NDTV Dialogues*, a show focusing on issues that have dropped off media and political discourse. In her over twenty-year career, Singh has hosted many award-winning shows, including *India Decides*, *Your Call* and *Verdict*. Singh has also successfully managed news ranging from the Kandahar hijack, the attack on the Parliament Houes, 26/11, the Vajpayee government's dramatic vote of confidence, Manmohan Singh as India's prime minister, the Gujarat riots and many other pivotal stories. She believes it is important to keep a sense of editorial perspective and take the long view of all that's happening around us in these turbulent times.

EARLY DAYS

As a young girl in school, I had a burning desire to be a crusading journalist. *Time* magazine and its journalists were my inspiration. TV wasn't an option at the time. I had never even watched the news on Doordarshan, though newsreaders like Salma Sultan were household names. At the time, doing a journalism course was unheard of, so I opted for a degree in English Literature at St Stephen's College which for some reason everyone interested in writing did. After graduating at the top of my class, I applied to *India Today*. While I waited for a reply, I met Prannoy and Radhika Roy, who were doing *The World This Week* on Doordarshan then, and joined them as a stopgap. Twenty two years later, I'm still here.

I was incredibly lucky to have had a chance to be part of the revolution in TV journalism in India. We began as a production company with a half-hour weekly international programme. Then, we progressed to a daily news bulletin on Doordarshan. Now we are 24/7 in English and Hindi, broadcast around the world.

FIRST BIG ASSIGNMENT

I started off logging interviews done by others. However, because the medium was so new, within a few months of my joining NDTV in 1992, I was offered a chance to report from Kashmir for *The World This Week*. It only fell into our bouquet of international news because the UN was debating the issue. I grabbed it with both hands and headed off to what was at that time a very different Kashmir, a state barricaded and under siege from within. I remember being told by a friendly jawan to move from the road where I was doing my first ever piece to camera. When I asked why, a simple reply came. 'Madam, *yahan* bomb *phenk sakte hain* (Madam, they may drop a bomb here).'

A TV camera from a private Indian news organization was a rare sighting in Srinagar then and I found many people eager to tell their stories. There were stories that we had to fight to air when I returned with DD, repeatedly telling us to ensure that nothing 'anti-national' goes on air. The stories obviously had an impact and I was sent back a few months later to cover the kidnapping of four foreign hostages by a little-known terrorist group. It was exciting stuff for a twenty-two-year-old and a brilliant learning experience. As NDTV went on to do national news, I covered anything and everything, from elections to air crashes, international stories to fires. Facing the camera was virtually second nature by then, so anchoring was the next step and a greater editorial role along with it.

LEARNING ON THE JOB

I never studied formal journalism, so I may well be the wrong person to ask if a formal course in journalism is required. Because my education was in English literature, I had the luxury of learning on the job from top journalists like Prannoy Roy and Radhika Roy. Radhika Roy, editorial head of NDTV, whose sense of ethics and journalistic honesty inspire me every day, has always been a role model for me. However, it is a competitive field now and I do think a formal course in journalism adds value. The key, however, is passion for the truth, for telling India's stories.

LANDMARK STORIES

The Jessica Lall murder case has many memories attached to it as well. There was huge frustration amongst those who had covered the story. After the verdict, along with the disbelief, there was a sense of resignation. In our daily news meeting, I asked the crime reporter at NDTV to speak to the then police commissioner on why they couldn't appeal the judgment, re-examine evidence—just do something. He sarcastically told her on the phone, 'Tell your editor not to speak to me. Speak to the president.' Those words got me thinking, why not do just that? We decided to do a signature petition to take to the then president, Dr A.P.J. Abdul Kalam. But it would take too long to get physical signatures, so the quickest option was SMS-es (this was the pre-Twitter era). To build awareness, we planned a candlelight rally at India Gate, with a special broadcast of the event. It was an idea which spread like wildfire, many channels imitated us and it changed the norms of TV reporting at the time. Most importantly, it made India (and me) realize that even an ordinary person within the media can challenge the system.

Another interesting case was that of the Aarushi Talwar murder where I interviewed the victim's mother just a day after her husband had been arrested for their daughter's murder. Again, it amazed me that so many people judged Nupur Talwar not by what she actually said but by the fact that she didn't break down on air. Coincidentally, it was her dead daughter's birthday on the day of the interview, a fact I found out during the conversation. As I spoke to her, I realized she was completely numb and traumatized.

As soon as the camera was switched off, her control snapped and she wept copiously in a corner of our TV studio. Yet, for people all that mattered was that she was 'a cold mother'. This was absolute rubbish and a reminder that the camera can often portray an image that is not necessarily the reality. In fact, I think that the media should not have handled the story the way it did and strongly believe that Aarushi's parents are not guilty.

A WORD OF ADVICE

My advice to TV journalists: The camera is your sword. Know the basics of filming. You should be able to operate a simple camera if needed. They aren't even those big, bulky cameras these days. Be Internet-savvy. For example, if you are working in NDTV, filing stories for ndtv.com is a major job too. Every channel has a website that is competing with the other channels, so content needs to be updated promptly. The barriers between mediums have broken down, so you must be equipped with all of these talents to succeed as a broadcast journalist.

The larger principles of journalism are the same whether you work for a newspaper, website or TV channel. My advice to aspiring journalists is that the truth is out there. It's your duty to get it. Don't see this as a profession but a vocation. What drives any journalist—whether they are print, online or television—is passion for the field. You may be on desk or a reporter, your hunger for news and your desire to tell stories are everything.

You need to have a nose for news. Stories can emerge from anywhere. They can come to your mind as you are talking to or listening to people. Also, remember that this isn't a nine-to-five job. News happens at any time.

Know your facts and do your research. Don't ask silly questions. It will look terrible if the person you are interviewing knows more than you do. Remember that the journalist is not the star of the story—the story is the star.

SHEREEN BHAN

Shereen Bhan has spent fifteen years closely tracking corporate, policy news and developments that have defined the world of business. A graduate from St Stephen's College, New Delhi, and a holder of a masters degree in communication studies from the Department of Communication, Pune University, Bhan has been producing and anchoring flagship news shows on CNBC-TV18 like *India Business Hour* and *What's*

Hot for over a decade. She is the anchor and editor of *Young Turks*, one of India's longest-running shows on entrepreneurs, that has also successfully built a niche category in business news programming. She is also the host of *Overdrive*, which has won the New Television Award for the Best Auto Show for three consecutive years. Bhan has broken a range of news stories that have redefined the Indian economic landscape in recent times—from Vodafone's play to acquire Hutch-Essar, to Bharti Airtel's attempts to woo South Africa's MTN, to Ikea's plans to enter the Indian retail arena. She also won the FICCI Woman of the Year award for her contribution to the media in 2005, and was named a Young Global Leader by the World Economic Forum.

EARLY DAYS

I graduated from St Stephen's College in New Delhi and then did my masters in film and communications at Pune. I was looking to be a documentary film-maker while in college. What really shaped my entry into the field of broadcast journalism was my first internship. It was with Synergy Communications. This is where I realized that I had a nose for news.

After my postgraduate study, I started working with UTV Communications under Karan Thapar. My first job involved assisting on the show *Hard Talk India* (for BBC) and producing shows for Nafisa Ali and Tavleen Singh. This experience gave me the grounding from research to lighting to organizing shoots. I learnt it all. Then in

2000, I was interviewed by the founders of TV18 for their soon-to-be-launched political channel. But twenty-four hours after the interview, Raghav Bahl, the founder of TV18, called me and asked me to join CNBC-TV18. I was apprehensive as I had no experience in business journalism but Raghav clearly believed in my abilities and decided to put me on air.

GOING THROUGH THE GRIND

I've done everything—production, research, editing, news shows, feature shows and anchoring. Sinking my teeth into it all has made me a versatile journalist who can deal with any issue that comes up on set or behind it. I've anchored every show on the channel. Today, I am the managing editor, looking after operations across India.

I have evolved along with the channel. I've kept pace with my interest in politics too. In fact, my beat has been business, policy and politics during my tenure here. I said yes to whatever came my way. Every challenge is a chance to learn something new. So I dabbled in everything while contributing across Network 18. I've anchored the CNN-IBN 8 p.m. programme and I've even anchored a show on CNBC Awaaz, our Hindi channel. My experience has been across channels and genres.

One plus point is that I have enthusiasm to take news head-on and am good at working with people. Being a broadcast journalist is not a lone-ranger job.

It is important to have the temperament to work with people and take them along. That is important to your success.

I have my idols in the TV industry. There's Prannoy Roy and Raghav Bahl here in India. They inspire any broadcast journalist striving to be at the top. Amongst those in TV abroad, I admire Oprah Winfrey for her tenacity. These people have invested a lot in their craft. Broadcast journalism is about digging your heels in and committing to perform.

HANDLING SUDDEN NEWS BREAKS

There are challenging days on a regular basis when you work on live television. We have to remain calm and poised in any situation. I remember the panic that spread across Mumbai when the 26/11 attacks happened. It was close to 9 p.m. when news started coming in, and I was at the EY entrepreneur awards in Mumbai. In fact, P.R.S. Oberoi, the chairman of the Oberoi Group, was there with us and even he had no idea of the attack at the Oberoi Hotel across town. We had very sketchy information on what was happening, so it was tough to organize our coverage plan. A journalist can't be trained for such a situation. You have to learn on the job. You are the public's link to the information so you can't falter.

Another challenging episode from my career occurred when the Left decided to support the 2004 UPA government. Left leader Sitaram Yechuri had demanded a complete ban on the disinvestment of profitable public sector undertakings (PSUs). I was a couple of years old in the business. The stock markets crashed fearing a rollback of reforms because of the Left party. I had to act quickly in getting clarifications from the government. All this was done in a matter of minutes. Being in broadcast news, the pace of events can sometimes be overwhelming.

A WORD OF ADVICE

My first piece of advice to aspiring TV news journalists is to learn that you can never say, 'I'll deal with it later.' I can't remember the last time I've switched off my phone. I've missed birthdays and family events often. This is *LIVE* TV. Personal sacrifice is a part of the drill.

Second, be open-minded. People often come in with notions about the business. These fixed ideas encourage them to believe that they should only work on a certain kind of show or do specific kinds of work. Thinking this way is doing a disservice to yourself. I remember my apprehension as I started with a genre unfamiliar to me, but if I had never been open to it, I wouldn't be where I am today. Be open to evolving and going with the flow.

And finally, don't forget that this medium is live. You must have the ability to think on your feet and respond immediately. The responsibility to put the news out accurately is yours. Take criticism, listen to feedback, read, and do your research.

Be innovative and creative. Push yourself. The TV medium requires this. It is a competitive medium. Think of yourself as a brand within the channel. Hone your skills and talent daily. Focus on your specialization but remain open to new challenges.

CHARUL MALIK

Charul Malik is a leading news anchor with fifteen years of experience in journalism. She began her journey from the local Citi channel in Chandigarh and then moved on the national news network Jain TV through an open audition. After that, she worked with Sahara for five years and then Star News (ABP News) for seven years. At ABP News, she was rated among the top female news anchors in the country. She covered diverse beats like politics, entertainment and sports. She was recognized by the Limca Book of Records for being the only news anchor to have done a live show on skates. She now anchors one of the most popular shows on Aaj Tak called *Saas Bahu Aur Betiya* and was awarded the NT Award for the Best Anchor in entertainment in 2014. Malik was nominated for the Asian Viewers Television Awards and the Indian Television Academy Awards for the best anchor in an entertainment and film-based show in 2014.

EARLY DAYS

As a child I was always fascinated with the news presenters on DD. Those were the days when Salma Sultan use to be the regular face as a news anchor. I was a talkative kid and would enjoy imitating her. I also made a habit of reading out loud the newspaper to my parents as if I was anchoring a show. Even today, my parents and twin sister are an integral part of what I do.

If you ask me, it is all right to formally study journalism before entering the field. But I hold a bachelors' degree and a law degree and didn't have any education in the subject. So what really matters is that you have the passion to achieve success. I believe that hard work and passion would make you learn on the job—better than any other way. The role of a broadcast journalist is not as easy and comfortable as it looks on screen. There is a lot of hard work that contributes toward the end product that viewers experience from their living rooms.

INITIAL SETBACK

I began my career with a rejection. I was just fifteen years old when I gave my first interview with Zee News. They rejected me saying that I had a long way to go. They even said that I was not journalist material. That incident inspired me to prove them wrong. I took on the challenge of working with my local city channel. Then I proceeded to give an open audition to Jain TV.

The audition was a success; I was selected and was asked to move to Delhi. This was where I began, thanks to support from the people who believed in me. I also want to thank people from Zee News for rejecting me, or else it wouldn't have pushed me to where I am now.

MEMORABLE ASSIGNMENTS

During my career, there have been numerous incidents that I have covered which have left a lasting impression in my mind and heart. One such incident occurred when I was covering the news of a small boy named Prince who had fallen into an open bore well and was rescued by the Indian Army. We continuously covered the news for around forty-nine hours without showing any emotions. My team and I felt the pain the family was going through. My own child was at a similar age then, so I knew how tough it was for them.

Another very interesting experience occurred while we were shooting for the Limca Book of Records during my stint with Star News (now ABP News). This programme was on air for nearly six months and we had to travel across India, meeting different record holders and asking them to perform their record-holding feats for the camera. (Since I was an anchor, I also performed some of the stunts with the record holders and that was acknowledged by the record book.) I anchored a live show while on skates, without falling down for close to an hour. I was interviewing Neil Nitin Mukesh and Deepika Padukone during their pre-run interview of the movie *Lafange Parinde* in which Deepika was playing a master skater. The entire experience taught me about chasing one's dreams with determination, dedication and hard work without losing focus.

LEARNING ON THE JOB

I also have experience in anchoring sports and religion-based shows. It took me little time to find out the difference in hosting these shows. For a sports show you should appear energetic, as if you are on the game field yourself. When you talk to analysts and experts, you have to have a certain lively pace of talking. And, of course, you need to have your background information correct such as number of runs (in case of cricket) and player history.

On the other hand, when I was the anchor of the show *Samarpan*, I remember the long broadcast of Varun Gandhi's wedding and how I had to know about all the religious customs of the ceremony. It was while I was on this show that a senior told me to talk in a more 'neutral' way to go with the subject of the show.

But, 'breaking news' requires a tone of urgency. Regular bulletins are another kind of challenge because you have to begin each one with fresh vigour, as if it is the first bulletin of the day—even if you have already read the same news twice.

When I think about idols on TV, Oprah Winfrey comes to mind. She's one of the few people I really look up to and follow closely. Not only is she a legend in her field, but she's also a true example of guts, focus and determination. Her life is not only an inspiration for me but for many who struggle in their daily lives. She is credited with promoting an intimate, confessional form of media communication, which has been borrowed by news entertainment shows across the globe. I aspire to meet her some day.

A WORD OF ADVICE

My advice to aspiring broadcast journalists is: Don't be impatient. People have big dreams. Everybody wants to be on camera but you cannot get there immediately. Even if you do a journalism course, there is no guarantee that your first job will have you on screen. Even if you become an anchor, you still need to be patient because you will go hours without a break and have to maintain the same energy level and alertness. If you're on the field as a reporter, you may face extreme conditions or discomforts, such as not having a toilet nearby. I believe that the amount of patience you have determines how good you'll be at your job.

Be a good listener. An anchor or a reporter must listen to the person he or she is talking to. If you zone out, you will miss crucial information that will result in gaps in your news story. Be alert. This means that you cannot let another news channel break a story before yours does. As a reporter, you need to keep your eyes open. Even if the breaking news is coming from a news agency like ANI or Reuters, you need to spot it first and get it.

SUHASINI HAIDAR

Suhasini Haidar is the diplomatic and strategic affairs editor of *The Hindu*, one of India's oldest and most respected national dailies. She has also been the presenter of the signature show *World View with Suhasini Haidar* on CNN-IBN. Haidar was foreign affairs editor and prime time anchor for India's leading twenty-four-hour English news channel CNN-IBN (2005–14) and correspondent for CNN International's New Delhi bureau. Over the course of her twenty-year reporting career, Haidar has reported under challenging circumstances in Pakistan, Sri Lanka, Libya, Lebanon and Syria. In India, she has covered the foreign affairs beat for over a decade and her domestic assignments include political profiles and in-depth reportage from conflict zones including Kashmir, where she was injured in a bomb blast in 2000. She was part of the CNN team that won the Columbia-Dupont Broadcast Journalism Award in 2005 for coverage of the tsunami in India, and worked for CNN.com in New York for a month during its 9/11 coverage.

EARLY DAYS

When I was in school, television news was not a career option. I grew up admiring newsreaders on Doordarshan, and may have heard BBC radio broadcasts that my parents tuned into, but I first only 'saw' broadcast journalism during the Gulf War, when CNN and BBC started to beam into India via satellite dishes. But while I marvelled at the courage of journalists who reported from the ground for the international channels, two things bothered me: one, that their reporting was fairly one-sided on the war, and the second, the reporters were almost always from Western countries.

In college (Delhi's Lady Shriram College), I studied statistics, expecting at that time that I would do an MBA and join the world of finance. I started applying to colleges here and in the US for their prospectuses. But a friend's offer to help produce a documentary really made me rethink what I wanted to study. On the one hand, the course lists on management theory and markets seemed dreary, while, on the other, the idea of covering news and working on films was magical. On a whim, almost, I applied to colleges in the US (no one taught broadcast journalism in India then), for a master's and got into Boston University. From that day in 1992, when I applied, till today, I haven't had a moment of regret!

I began my career, as most television journalists do, with an internship, when I was accepted by CNN in New York for the summer of 1994. My boss then, the UN correspondent for CNN, Richard Roth is still there, and as he liked my work, the internship extended into a job. I should have been ecstatic then, a twenty-one-year-old with an international television career ahead! But it wasn't the US market that I wanted to work in. So, despite advice to the opposite from my professors at Boston University and some of my family, I returned to India, where channels like NDTV and Zee were just making their mark. I did many interviews, but surprisingly, none of them would hire me. After about six months of freelancing and tossing about (I even did a short stint for Mexican TV), the CNN New Delhi bureau chief got in touch. Their producer was going on maternity leave, and I could fill-in for her for the year.

REPORTING FROM CONFLICT ZONES

Every day in the profession has taught me something, and that's why I still wake up every morning wondering what's in store. My early years at CNN opened my mind to covering stories from all sides, my travels took me to neighbouring countries I had never been to: Pakistan at the height of India–Pakistan tensions, Sri Lanka during some of the worst times of the war and LTTE terrorism, Bangladesh at the peak of violent political hartals, and all the rest. But we spent the most time travelling to Kashmir, as it was in the throes of militancy. We also saw some of the brutality of security forces, and the complete barbarism of the terrorists.

Once, I was the only person in the bureau, when video arrived of a hostage who had been killed. I put it on and nearly fainted, as there was his body, severed at the head, which had been placed in his hands. Journalists in Srinagar in those days were targeted in different ways. While we were constantly under surveillance from the government, we also realized that militant groups would follow us around, seeing what we reported on. Sometimes, a militant commander would contact us to do an interview, and those encounters are the stuff of a different essay. When we would come back from such assignments, or covered a village where there had been violence, we would get a visit from intelligence officers, admonishing and threatening us. I thought we were doing our job, and would say so. But even though the situation looked bad for the government, the militants knew they were losing the battle. They got more desperate.

After twenty-five years of excitement on television front lines, I can really ask for no more than such truly exciting anecdotes, great friendships and partnerships in the field, and the satisfying memories of a job well done—most of the time at least!

A WORD OF ADVICE

I meet, speak with, and get Twitter messages everyday from aspiring broadcast journalists, who feel disheartened about not finding a job, or about not getting assignments and the like. All I can say to them is, 'Keep the faith and be true to your journalism.' Broadcast journalism will give you all the breaks you work hard for, to the point you will soon complain about too much work, and not enough sleep! What is also important is how well you sleep at night, and if you are true to your journalism, honest to your story, and refuse to make convenient compromises with the truth, you won't have any problem sleeping at all, exhausted, but exhilarated too.

15

Important Websites

Check out these websites. The 'Contact Us' or 'Careers' section will usually have information that you need. And remember that getting familiar with an organization helps you ace the interview.

Major English news networks

NDTV	www.ndtv.com
Times Now	http://www.timesnow.tv
CNBC-TV18	http://www.moneycontrol.com/cnbctv18
Headlines Today	http://headlinestoday.intoday.in
Doordarshan News	www.ddinews.gov.in
CNN-IBN	http://ibnlive.in.com

Major Hindi news networks

Aaj Tak	http://aajtak.intoday.in

ABP News	http://www.abplive.in
ZEE News	http://zeenews.india.com
India TV	http://www.indiatvnews.com
Doordarshan News	http://ddinews.gov.in/Hindi/pages/default.aspx
IBN 7	http://khabar.ibnlive.in.com
CNBC Awaaz	http://hindi.moneycontrol.com/tv

News Agencies

Asian News International (ANI)	http://www.aniin.com
Press Trust of India (PTI)	http://www.ptinews.com
Associated Press (AP)	http://www.ap.org
Reuters	http://in.reuters.com

Others

Ministry of Information and Broadcasting	http://mib.nic.in
News Broadcasters Association	http://www.nbanewdelhi.com

16

Sample CVs

Sample CV 1

Sue Patel, 149B, Golf Club Road
Kolkata-700045
Email: suepatel@gmail.com, Mobile: 9999900000

Objective: To work in a TV newsroom and learn how things work there.

Summary of Skills: Reporting news and features as a print journalist, writing grammatical English, public speaking, debating, taking on leadership roles, understanding people in a sociological context.

Educational Qualifications

Bachelor of Arts in English (First Class)	St Stephen's College, Delhi	2014
A Levels[1] in English (A), Sociology (B) and History (B)	Calcutta International School	2011

1 The General Certificate of Education Advanced *Level* (GCE Advanced Level), or more commonly, the *A Level*, is a school leaving qualification offered by educational bodies in the United Kingdom and the British Crown dependencies. In India, GCE Advanced Level qualifications are offered at private and international schools as an alternative to the conventional Indian School Certificate (ISC) programme.

Extra-curricular Activities

School debate team captain	2009–2011
Reporter on the college newspaper	2012–2014
Public speaking	2013–2014

Internship Experience

Three-month internship at City TV	May 2014–August 2014

Learnt how the newsroom works. Reported on local events. Learnt how to do research for news stories and the basics of writing a script.

Awards

Winning team captain of inter-school debate competition	2010 and 2011
First prize in inter-college public speaking competition	2013

Languages Known: English, Bengali, Hindi.

Web Presence

- My blog suepwrites.wordpress.com is updated weekly with posts about books I'm reading or movies that I've watched.
- I tweet at @suepwrites

Interests

- Outside of the classroom and my extra-curricular activities, I volunteer my time at an old-age home. When I am there, I help serve the elderly food and read books to them.
- I took tennis lessons as a child and still play once a week at least.

- I watch a lot of movies and read books which I then review on my blog.

References: Available upon request.

Sample CV 2

Ravi Mohapatra
48, Garden Road
Flat 5A
Bhubaneswar-751008
Email: ravim90@yahoo.com
Mobile: 9393939393

Objective: An entry-level job in TV journalism with a keen interest in reporting. To work in the country's top TV news channel and master all the techniques of production, news writing and editing as I grow there.

Summary of Skills: Public speaking, debating, fundamental knowledge of broadcast journalism and the newsroom, elementary new production techniques, scriptwriting, video editing.

Educational Qualifications

Postgraduate diploma in Broadcast Journalism (First class)	Indian Institute of Journalism and New Media, Bengaluru	2014
Masters degree in English (First class)	Ravenshaw University, Cuttack	2013
Bachelors degree in English (First Class)	Ravenshaw University, Cuttack	2010

Extra-curricular Activities

Public speaking	2010–2013
Photography	2010–2013

Awards

Second in inter-college public speaking competition	2012 and 2013
Best photographer prize in university photography competition	2013

Languages Known: English, Oriya, Hindi.

Web Presence

- I blog at ravijourno.wordpress.com. The blog is like my own newspaper where I write about things happening around my hometown and campus. My posts are about everything starting from a local festival to a fire.
- My twitter handle is @ravijourno; I tweet links to my blog and interesting news articles.
- I am on Instagram at @ravi. my photographs tell stories of people and animals in Orissa.

Interests

- I have been playing the guitar since my childhood, and still do.
- I volunteer at an animal shelter for a few months every year.

References: Available upon request.

The candidate with Sample CV 1 was placed as a trainee editor at a regional TV news channel. She started by getting her hands dirty at the output desk.

The candidate with Sample CV 2 joined a national TV network in New Delhi as a correspondent. His job involved covering stories from all beats. After two years, he joined a news agency and reported from all over the country.

17

ARE YOU READY TO ROLL?

By now I hope you've figured out the dynamics of a bustling newsroom. You even have a detailed breakdown of the various jobs and skills one needs to carry them out. Now the crucial, looming question: 'Do you fit the bill?' Go through this check list and see if you're up for the challenge.

CAN YOU MEET STRICT DEADLINES?

Whether you're the reporter on the field or the producer in the newsroom, there will always be a time crunch in the field of TV journalism. The news is unpredictable. You should just know that sooner or later in your day, you will be rushing to get things ready. Sometimes reporters need to travel far away to cover a story, and get back to the station with enough time to write the script and edit the video. Producers must make sure they're putting out the most recent and important news. Sometimes this means changing the news report queue with just seconds to spare.

CAN YOU HANDLE STRESSFUL SITUATIONS?

Not everything is pleasant in the news industry. Even if you are doing a story about summer that includes mangoes and iced tea, chances are that you will endure some level of stress. As a reporter, you will eventually need to face a story that will not only tug at your heartstrings, but also make you witness things you've never seen before. For example, covering a murder or stampede can be overwhelming. If you are involved in production, you may not personally witness stressful incidents, but will still have to handle tense situations in the office.

CAN YOU TALK TO EVERYONE?

The news is about everything that's going on in your community and around the world. That's why people that work in the news often have to extract their information and interviews from all sorts of people—from the mayor to restaurant owners to homeless people to company CEOs. Broadcast journalists, both on the field and in the newsroom, need to be able to communicate with people from all walks of life.

CAN YOU MULTI-TASK?

Juggling many tasks at the same time is not uncommon for people that work in the newsroom. Reporters usually need to cover more than one story at a time, videographers have to edit various pieces, producers are in charge of managing multiple stories, and directors must oversee the entire process from start to finish. Broadcasting is right for you only if you can handle multiple things and still conduct interviews and look good on camera. Putting a news show on air is a complex process which requires all the components of the team to be in sync with each other. Thus, multi-tasking is a crucial skill in broadcast journalism.

DO YOU FEEL COMFORTABLE WITH TECHNOLOGY?

We all know that in this day and age technology changes faster than the blink of an eye. The newest gadget of today will be replaced by a superior one tomorrow. Being in the field of broadcast, you will need to move with the times. A typical newsroom contains dozens of computers, news production systems, editing software, many kinds of digital tapes, converters, recording devices, cameras and screens. Broadcast journalism is essentially a technology-based field, so you need to be gadget-friendly.

CAN YOU KEEP YOUR COMPOSURE?

On air, reporters are expected to maintain a professional attitude even in the most stressful of situations. In the studio, producers must keep their cool even in the midst of a newsroom crisis. All aspects of broadcast journalism require the need to keep calm. In order to best communicate your message to viewers, you should be able to sound confident, alert and informed.

So, what do you think? Is the TV newsroom the place for you? If you know you can handle all of these challenges, you're ready to begin your career. Good luck!

Glossary

Ad lib	Unrehearsed, unscripted action or speech
Agency or wire copy	News material received from news agencies
Angle	Short for 'news angle'; the aspect a journalist decides to highlight and develop
Beat	Field or topic that a reporter reports on
Clip	Any piece of film or tape that is taken out from a sequence to use elsewhere
Close-up	Shot which focuses on one detail (e.g., face or arm)
Communication satellite	Man-made device in space that passes television signals between globe locations
Copy	Written material for news

Correspondent	Journalist who reports on a special subject or from a particular location
Depth of focus	Distance between the TV lens and the subject of the camera
Documentary	An hour-long or half-hour-long report on a single topic
Dry run	Rehearsal without a camera
Editing	Joining pictures together/fixing scripts for language and style
Fade in	Camera effect or graphics effect where an image slowly disappears or appears into darkness
Feed	Transmission of stories to a station by a network or news agency service through a special telephone line or satellite
Flash	News/breaking news information that is flashed at the bottom of the TV screen
Follow-up	News report based on previously broadcast material
Footage	Preserved shots
Genre	A type of news story or programme that can be categorized for style and purpose
Grab	Frame of video footage

Graphics	TV artwork
Hard news	Serious news
Head shot	Close-up of face
Jargon	Specialized language concerned with a particular profession or subject
Key shot	Master shot
Kill	To cut or remove action, lines or stories
Lead	Opening item of a newscast
Long shot	Shot taken from a distance to show the whole scene
Live	Direct transmission of action as it happens
OB van	Outdoor broadcast van
Out cue	Last words on a sound bite or VO
Overexposure	When too much light enters the frame and gives a washed-out effect
Package	Completed television news story pre-prepared for a news bulletin and ready for transmission. A package will contain a written introduction for the newsreader, the reporter's edited report complete with vision and sound and an out cue for the end

Pan	To move the camera horizontally while the pedestal remains stationary
Piece to camera (PTC)	Reporter speaking to anchor from spot of incident/news story
Portfolio	Folder or videotape containing samples of your work
Resolution	Degree to which fine detail in the image can be distinguished
Rundown	Outline of a programme or part of a programme; includes the list of stories to be heard, in order
Run-through	Rehearsal
Shot	Series of pictures of a happening
Soft news	Features on genres such as health or gadgets that are added for entertainment
Sound bite	Short extract from a recorded interview or speech
Still	Single picture
Storyboard	Drawing of video next to audio in a fashion that details all elements of a programme; a visual script
Stringer	A freelance contributor
Take	Each time a shot is filmed or recorded

Ticker	Texts that run at the bottom of the screen giving news updates
VO or Voice-over	Commentary spoken by an unseen reader
Zoom-in	Reducing the angle of view by increasing the focal length of a zoom lens during a shot causing subject to become larger
Zoom-out	Increasing the angle of view to make subject look smaller

References

Books

Kaushik, Sharda. *Script to Screen: An Introduction to TV Journalism*, New Delhi: Trinity Press, 2014.

Pande, Navodita. *TV Journalism*, New Delhi: APH Publishing Corporation, 2012.

Shrivastava, K.M. *Broadcast Journalism in the 21st Century*, Delhi: Sterling Publishers Pvt. Ltd, 2013.

Singh, Rajesh K. *Broadcast Journalism Techniques of News Writing, Reporting and Production*, New Delhi: Manglam Publications, 2010.

Wainwright, David. *Journalism Made Simple*, New Delhi: Rupa & Co., 1992.

Thompson, Robert, and Cindy Malone. *The Broadcast Journalism Handbook: A Television News Survival Guide*, Washington, DC, Rowman & Littlefield, 2004.

WEBSITES

http://www.bbc.co.uk/blogs/legacy/theeditors/2006/06/what_does_an_editor_do.html

http://www.indianetzone.com/42/news_agencies_india.htm www.spj.org

http://media.about.com/od/televisionandradio/p/Tv-News-Director-Career-Profile.htm

http://www.educationtimes.com/article/246/2011081320110813184313565cacd9f04/Tell-a-News-Story.html

http://tvnewsmodule.blogspot.in/2005/12/history-indian-broadcast-journalism.html

http://prndg.org/job-description-news-director

http://www.internationalstudent.com/study-broadcasting/is-broadcasting-right-for-you

http://xperiencemedia.blogspot.in/2009/02/difference-between-broadcast-and-print.html

http://www.prospects.ac.uk/television_camera_operator_job_description.htm

http://indiatoday.intoday.in/itmi/

http://www.iijnm.org/broadcast-journalism.htm

http://www.educationtimes.com/article/100/2009102720091027155524578446d6f3/News-breakers.html

http://www.iimc.nic.in/training-pg-journalism-radio-television.html

http://www.asianmedia.org/streams/television.asp

http://ftiindia.com/

http://webershandwickindia.com/digital-life-indian-journalists/

http://www.thenewsmanual.net

http://www.caravanmagazine.in/vantage/television-scripted

http://www.dnaindia.com/india/report-mass-media-biased-towards-anna-hazares-cause-experts-1580587

APPENDIX

Sample from Indian Institute of Journalism and New Media Website

Welcome to the exciting, entertaining, and informative world of broadcast journalism. Through this programme you will discover and master the best techniques of reporting, writing and editing broadcast news stories. You will learn the basics of television and radio skills, shoot and record interviews, plan and execute news stories, and also get an insight into nuances of editing and news presentation techniques.

Students of television journalism will also be involved in regular course work as reporters, camera-persons, editors, writers and producers, using highly sophisticated TV production equipment and editing and production software. Radio journalism students will discover the magic of the medium—and its endless possibilities of online radio and podcasts.

Students of radio journalism will be involved in regular course work as reporters, editors, writers and producers, using sophisticated equipment and audio-editing software. Students will learn radio production skills, reporting stories as well as reporting live events, organizing and moderating discussions and interviews. Students will also be exposed to the nuances of the medium and to the aesthetics of mixing and editing various forms of audio—music, voice, sound effects, etc.

The programme will incorporate the following core courses:

- *Reporting and Writing Broadcast (Television and Radio)*
- *Tools of Television/Radio Journalism*
- *Advanced Television/Radio Studies*
- *Television/Radio News Bulletin and Documentary*
- *Television/Radio Workshop*
- *Ethical and Legal Issues in Journalism*
- *Convergence across Media*
- *Critical Thinking in Journalism*
- *Liberal Arts*

Acknowledgements

This book could not have taken shape without Amrita Chowdhury's help. She had suggestions and feedback that added the polish that my manuscript needed at every step.

Debasri Rakshit and the HarperCollins team deserve a special thank you for turning my manuscript into a beautiful book. I also thank Mohini Chaudhuri for putting in immense effort as my editor.

And last, but not the least, I thank all the journalists from across India for giving me their valuable time and insights. The book would not have been possible without their enthusiastic participation.

A big thank you to: Vaibhav Varma, Angshuman Deb Barma, Saurabh Gupta, Manish Batavia, Jayeeta Ganguly, Sambit Pal, Ajay Sharma, Naomi Datta, Ritu Singh, Ranveer Singh and Professor Mrinal Chatterjee.